TYPICAL JAPANESE COOKING

TOMI EGAMI

translated by V. A. McKenzie Skillman

PHOTO by YOSHIKATSU SAEKI

COPYRIGHT, ©, 1959, BY TOMI EGAMI
LIBRARY OF CONGRESS CATALOG CARD NUMBER : 59–14423
First Edition 1959

Publisher:
SHIBATA PUBLISHING CO., LTD.
2, 3-Chome, Hongo, Bunkyo-ku, Tokyo, Japan

Exclusive distributors :
JAPAN PUBLICATIONS TRADING CO., LTD.
Central P. O. Box 722, Tokyo, Japan

Printed in Japan

Preface

When I was in France studying at the École de Cuisine Le Cordon Bleu and after that in England, I came to appreciate the culinary arts of those countries as well as those of twenty-six others through which I have traveled. Nevertheless, I feel that the Japanese dinner is unique and it is with much pleasure that I see information about Japanese cooking presented to the world.

The characteristics of the Japanese dinner, as I see it, are 1) the quiet appeal of natural beauty in delicious food which dedicated cooks produce; 2) the dishes which match the mood and appearance of the food; 3) the flavor of soy sauce, the singular seasoning of Japanese origin, which is most palatable and satisfying.

It is the intention of this book to present to its readers in as simple a form as possible some of the cooking of my country. At the same time I realize that the symbolism represented by the way in which the food is prepared may be difficult to understand.

It is my hope that this book will be of service to its readers in experiencing the joy of successful preparation of Japanese dishes using available products.

Much appreciation is hereby given to Mr. Yasuyoshi Tasaki and Mrs. John (Verlie Anne) Skillman for their kind assistance.

June, 1959

Tomi Egami

Contents

1. The recipes in this book make 5 servings except where otherwise indicated.
2. Before making the recipes, please look at the section on " How to make soup stock ". All the soup stock recipes have been numbered and these numbers inserted into other recipes for your convenience.
3. Some of the foods in this book will be unavailable in foreign countries except as canned products. We have tried to designate these foods by this sign∗.
4. The following abbreviations are used in this book.
   lb. (s) = pound (s)
   oz. (s) = ounce (s)
   T. = American tablespoon
   t. = American teaspoon
   pkg. = package
   in. = inch
5. Measurement equivalents
   1 lb. = 454 gr.
   1 oz. = 28.35 gr.
   1 cup = 16 T. = 8 ounce (Japan $1^1/_5$ cups)
   1 T. = 3 t. (Japan   1 T.)
   1 t. = (Japan   1 t.)

Raw Fish
Spring Fish Festival

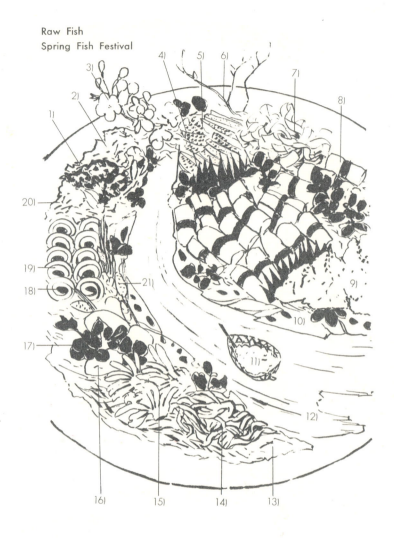

1)	yellow flower (spring)	12)	*kanten*
2)	radish	13)	cucumber
3)	cherry flower	14)	snipe fish
4)	*haran*	15)	cockle fish
5)	sea bream	16)	pebble
6)	willow tree twig	17)	*bofu* leaf
7)	spikenard	18)	*nori* seaweed
8)	tuna fish	19)	cuttlefish
9)	cuttlefish with egg yolk	20)	radish
10)	lotus root	21)	cat tail
11)	horseradish or *wasabi*		

A GLIMPSE OF JAPANESE COOKING

Japan is a long island country lying between the 30th and 45th parallels, surrounded by the Pacific Ocean on her east and by the Sea of Japan on her west. The country is very small in area but its great length from north to south gives it a variety of climates, with the northern tip being two months behind its southern counterpart in temperature. Added to this wide variety are the climatic changes brought about by the cold and warm currents that touch the country's coasts with the changes in seasons. Thanks to this climatic boon, Japan can enjoy almost every variety of food usually found from subtropical to frigid zones.

Japan's Climate and her Produce

As the country is small in size, it is very easy to transport these varieties of foods from one place to another, giving us the opportunity to enjoy practically every choice dish there is at a minimum cost. They range from vegetables, fruits, fish and shellfish, lobsters, crabs, cereals to animal and bird meat. Japan is especially proud of her delicious marine products as the country is completely surrounded by sea. Marine products therefore, have long been an integral part of Japanese life and we cannot think of any truly Japanese dinner without fish or shellfish dishes. Japan can also be proud of her vegetables. My business takes me far and wide in the outside world, but never have I seen a country endowed with a greater variety of vegetables and to me, the Japanese are the best cooks of vegetables and fruits.

Given this wide variety of sea foods and vegetables that colorfully rotate with the seasons, it has become a trade mark of Japanese hospitality to treat one's friends to dishes of the "firsts" of the season both at home and at restaurants.

Varieties of Japanese Cooking Methods

There are many methods of Japanese cooking and it is next to impos-

1

sible to make rough generalizations. However, you can usually group minor differences into 5 broad categories. They are: 1) *Yushiki Ryori* (Court Dishes); 2) *Kaiseki Ryori* (Party Dishes); 3) *Gishiki Ryori* (Ceremony Dishes); 4) *Kaiseki Ryori* (Tea Ceremony Dishes; not to be confused with the first *Kaiseki Ryori*); and 5) *Katei Ryori* (Household Dishes). Now I will give a brief description of the above 5 kinds of dishes.

1) *Yushiki Ryori* (Court Dishes) *Yushiki Ryori* was born out of the Imperial Court during the *Nara* Period (710–787) and has been practiced among the courtiers. It is not in practice now except on very special occasions.

2) *Kaiseki Ryori* (Party Dishes) *Kaiseki Ryori* is meant for entertaining one's friends Its first requirement is that one's friends can enjoy the dishes with Japanese *sake*. Every dish in this method is so designed that the *sake* is highlighted. This method has been so popular with the Japanese and so frequently utilized, that some foreigners consider quite mistakenly that this is the only kind of Japanese cooking in existence. However, this is only a part of the abundant variety.

3) *Gishiki Ryori* (Ceremony Dishes) As the name suggests, *Gishiki Ryori* is served on occasions of either celebration or mourning. Especially gorgeous are the celebration dishes. They are so abundant in volume and variety that the members of the ceremony have to take most of the dishes home with them.

4) *Kaiseki Ryori* (Tea Ceremony Dishes) *Kaiseki Ryori* is a direct offspring of the traditional Japanese tea ceremony. Every dish and the vessel on which it is served conform strictly to the taste of a *chajin* (tea ceremony master). This is representative of *Kyoto* Dishes.

5) *Katei Ryori* (Household Dishes) *Katei Ryori* are side dishes eaten with the traditional Japanese boiled rice. As a result they are usually very highly seasoned and differ in contents and volume from home to home.

Japanese tableware is very different from both those of the Western countries and those of other Asian countries. Unlike other countries, there is no custom in Japan of diners helping themselves from a large dish placed in the center of the table. (It is true that in recent years, especially after the Pacific War, the influence of Western and Chinese cooking has led the Japanese to use serving plates more often.) Japan's speciality is to use many small dishes for each of the members and to make the dishes small objects of art. It is here especially that the Japanese cook puts his heart in his work. Sometimes 2 or 3 kinds of food are served in the same dish to

2

give it color and symmetry.

Foreigners often say Japanese dishes are feasts to the eye rather than to the stomach. In a way, this is quite true. We are often dumbfounded by the beauty and symmetry of Japanese dishes served in small artistic vessels. It is deemed especially important to the Japanese to serve a particular food in dishes of the same color, pattern and shape, however many their guests may be.

These dishes, put on small vessels, are usually served to the guests on small tables called *zen*. Each member of the party is served with a *zen*. They do not eat on the same big table as in the case of Western dinners. The *zen* has 4 legs, the length of which varies from a very small 4 centimeters to 25 centimeters. Recently this kind of dinner is falling out of popularity among the Japanese, however, possibly because of its ostentatiousness and complexity and is served only for a very big party or for foreigners who want to see Japan at its traditional best. A short-legged, rather big table is usually set up for a small party or for household guests for common use. Hosts will place various dishes on this table and when they want to be especially courteous, they place the abovementioned miniature tables on the common table and serve the dishes on them.

Seasonings in Japanese Cooking

Just as soup stock is the base of all Western dishes, a clear soup made of *konbu* seaweed, dried young sardines and water is the base of all Japanese dishes. Other seasonings include soy sauce, sugar, salt, vinegar, *miso* soy bean paste, oil and *sake*. Soy sauce, queen of the Japanese seasonings, is a salty brown liquid made of wheat, soy beans and salt. Soy sauce is loved by the Japanese people for its flavor and almost no dish is conceivable without it.

The exception to the above rule is the *Kaiseki Ryori* No. 1, which is meant to be only an accompanyment to *sake* or *mirin*. In the *Kaiseki Ryori*, the use of soy sauce is greatly toned down to keep the flavor of the dishes as delicate as possible. In this case, salt takes the place of soy sauce. It is in *Katei Ryori* (household dishes) that soy sauce comes into its own, as these dishes are meant to be eaten with the fairly tasteless boiled rice.

Next in line in importance to soy sauce is *miso* soy bean paste, which is made of soy beans and rice or wheat. Unless there is a false step in its making, *miso* soy bean paste lasts for several years without deterioration. *Miso* soy bean paste is a very handy seasoning for Japanese households, as

3

it can be used with almost any materials including fish, meat, or vegetables. *Miso* soy bean paste can be used not only as a seasoning but as a main dish. In olden times, when transportation was inadequate, people in the country districts relied on *miso* soy bean paste for their protein intake. Even at present, *miso* soy bean paste is one of the most versatile of all Japanese foods.

Kinds of Japanese Dishes and the Way to Serve Them

There is so much variety in Japanese dishes that it is next to impossible to explain them all. I will deal with only the most popular ones here in the order they are served in a regular Japanese dinner.

1) *Zensai* (Hors d'Oeuvre) *Zensai* is just the same in purpose and appeal to the Western hors d'oeuvre. It is cold and appetizing. The only difference is that there is much less volume in the Japanese hors d'oeuvre than in its Western counterpart.

2) *Shirumono* (Soup) *Shirumono* correspond to Western soups. Roughly, they are 2 kinds of Japanese soups; one clear and the other thick. The former consists of soup stock made from *konbu* seaweed, dried young sardine and slightly seasoned fish, shrimp or chicken plus seasonal vegetables. The latter, the thick soup is made of soup stock and liquidized *miso* soy bean paste. Added to this base are vegetables, chicken or pork, fish and shellfish. The thick soup is usually called *miso* soup and is eaten every morning by the majority of Japanese. Slightly different but still basically a soup, is *chawan-mushi*. This is made of egg custard with a soup base and steamed in a cup with slices of vegetables and chicken. This is a favorite Japanese dish among foreigners.

3) *Sashimi* (Raw Fish) *Sashimi* is truly a Japanese dish. Some foreigners shudder at the mere mention of eating raw fish. But I think they are missing a lot. *Sashimi* is actually slices of raw fish cut out of fresh raw fish, lobster, or cuttlefish and it is eaten with grated *wasabi* horseradish, grated radish, or thin pieces of *udo* (a sort of asparagus) to make the fish meat more digestible.

4) *Kuchitori* or *Moriawase* (Special Occasion Side Dish) This dish is a combination of 2 or 3 cold foods arranged in an artistic order. It is one of the most beautifully executed dishes in Japan.

5) *Hachizakana* (Broiled Dish) Broiled fish, chicken, pork, lobsters, eels and others are often called *Hachizakana Ryori*. Seasonings and the

4

method of broiling differ from item to item and they can be broiled to individual tastes.

6) *Nimono* (Boiled Food) *Nimono* is usually based on seasonal vegetables plus soy sauce and sugar seasoning. Sometimes added to this are chickens, lobsters, fish, crabs, bird meat, shellfish and seaweed.

7) *Chuzara* *Chuzara* is a kind of dish served in relatively big dishes or in covered dishes. It consists of fried fish or vegetables, or steamed. Soy bean curd is used frequently.

8) *Sunomono* or *Aemono* (Salad) *Sunomono* or *aemono* is seaweed, shellfish, lobsters and chicken prepared with vinegar, salt, sugar and other seasonings together with those vegetables in season. Often such things as ground sesame seeds, or grated walnuts are added to give color. Materials are usually fresh but sometimes cooked materials are used or added.

9) If your guests like *sake*, you should provide them with some from time to time all through the courses. When they finish *sunomono*, they should be given boiled rice together with *miso* soup and pickles. If your guests do not care for drinks, you should provide them with boiled rice from the start of the courses.

The number of dishes served varies surprisingly from one occasion to another. Japanese provide many dishes when they have guests at their table. However, they have few dishes when there are no guests.

Japanese Way of Cooking and its Features

Smallness can be said to be one of the most important characteristics of the Japanese way of cooking. Each item is cut into small and thin pieces just as in the case of the *sengiri* (cut into strips), often used in Japanese dishes. With chicken, for example, Japanese cooks pry the meat completely off the bones and cut it into small pieces. The deftness of Japanese cooks plays a big hand here. Especially wonderful is their technique in cutting and peeling vegetables. They deserve the name of "magicians of cutlery". A real cook has scores of knives, big and small, at his finger tips. True cooks pay great attention to the size and shape of the pans and bowls they use in their cooking. They are very careful in their preparation and seasoning of foods—each item tailored to individual tastes.

As elsewhere mentioned, the purely Japanese dishes specialize in fresh,

5

raw materials with a minimum use of oils and fats. They also avoid grease and strong spices, using only delicate and fragrant seasonings. This is mainly because most of the materials found in Japan have fresh and delicate flavors and are more colorful in appearance when raw. Japanese love to savour these features to the full.

When seated before the table, Japanese use chopsticks to eat the food served on many small dishes. They rarely use knives at the table, as there are no big dishes in the center of the table for common carving. Also they rarely use seasonings after the dishes are already served, unless they come with the dishes. It is common both in Western countries and in Japan that good manners call for polite and beautiful handing of everything on the table.

(Reprinted from ; *The Oriental Economist*, July, 1958)

Party Dishes

1) rice	7) wan Japanese soup bowl
2) boiled food	8) soy sauce
3) raw fish	9) *sakazuki* wine cup
4) *hachi zakana*	10) chopsticks
5) *sake*	11) chopstick rest
6) hors d'oeuvre	

KAISEKI RYORI, PARTY DISHES

1. *Zatsuki*, **Hors d'Oeuvre**

At the first course of the dinner each guest has a tray placed before him with chopsticks placed on the chopstick rest, *sakazuki* wine cup and a dish of hors d'oeuvre. See figure 1. It is known as an individual table or tray, *zatsuki-zen*. (In a more informal occasion the second course of clear soup may be added to the first course.) See figure 2. *Sake*, rice wine is served constantly throughout the meal and it is warmed to 110°–140°F before serving.

2. *Suimono*, **Clear Soup**

The clear soup is placed in the center of the small table before the hors d'oeuvre is finished, if it is not served with the first course. (See figure 2.)

3. *Mukozuke*, **Raw Fish**

The dish of raw fish is brought to the table and placed on the far side of the bowl of clear soup. The guest is supposed to put used dishes on the rice mat floor beside the tray, when he is finished so they will not be in the way. The waiter will remove them from there, or from the tray if the guest wishes. (See figure 3.)

4. *Kuchitori*, **Special Occasion Side Dish**

By this time the soup will be finished and the dish set on the floor with the dish of raw fish still to be eaten. The raw fish dish is pushed to the right to give way to the special occasion side dish which is now served in the center. (See figure 4.)

5. *Hachi Zakana*, **Broiled Dish**

This is served in the spot occupied by the special occasion side dish which is now pushed to the right with the raw fish dish put on the floor to be removed by the waiter. (See figure 5.)

6. *Nimono*, **Boiled Food**

In a similar manner this dish comes in the middle of the table with

7

the broiled food dish on the right and the special occasion side dish put on the floor to be removed by the waiter. (See figure 6.)

7. *Sunomono*, **Salad**

The salad is placed on the upper right with the boiled food dish in the center and the broiled food dish put on the floor to be removed by the waiter. (See figure 7.)

8. *Shiizakana*, **Entrée**

This dish is placed in the center and the boiled food dish put on the floor. (See figure 8.) Fried foods, special salads, etc. make up this course.

9. **Rice,** *Miso* **Soup and Pickle**

When this course is brought in the table is cleared of dishes including wine cup, but the entrée may remain if unfinished. Thus the table is re-arranged with the rice bowl on the left hand side, the *miso* soup on the right hand and the pickle at the far side from the guest. (See figure 9.)

10. *Bancha*, **Green Tea**

The guests drink the tea in the same bowl in which the rice was served after the rice is finished. There are many kinds of green tea. *Bancha* tea is made from the less tender leaves and is considered inferior to *sencha* which is made from the youngest tenderest tea leaves. *Matcha* is used for the tea ceremony and is bitter, very expensive and considered the most delicious tea.

11. **Fruit**

When the tea is finished, the table is removed and seasonal fruit is served on individual plates in front of each person.

12. **Dessert and Tea**

As a final course, a lacquer ware dish is used for dessert. The dessert can be one of 3 special kinds; one is made of *mochi* rice (*mochi gashi*); one is made of steamed sweets (*mushi gashi*); and the third often is made of red bean paste (which spoils quickly, therefore the name is *nama gashi*). *Sencha* or *matcha* is served with the dessert.

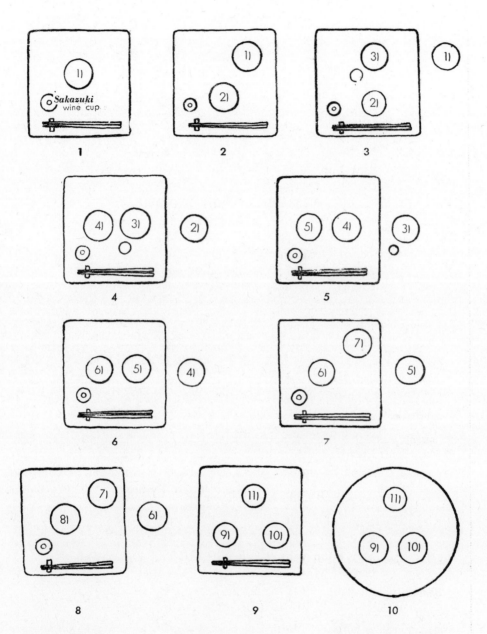

1) hors d'oeuvre   2) *suimono*, clear soup   3) *mukozuke*, raw fish

4) *kuchitori*, special occasion side dish   5) *hachizakana*, broiled dish

6) *nimono*, boiled food   7) *sunomono*, salad   8) *shiizakana*, entrée

9) rice   10) *miso* soup   11) pickle

The Menu of *Kaiseki* (Party Dishes)

Hors d'Oeuvre
> Spiced Chicken

Suimono, Clear Soup
> Egg Custard   Spinach
>> Japanese Pepper Sprout

Mukozuke, Raw Fish
> Checker Fish
>> Radish   *Ugu*   *Metade*
>>> *Wasabi*, Horseradish
>>> Daffodil

Kuchitori, Special Occasion Side Dish
> *Hakata* Tomato, Tomato and Egg Sandwich
> Chicken *Oharame*
> Bracken with Soy Bean Curd Dressing

Hachizakana, Broiled Dish
> Bamboo Shoots and Eel Sandwich
>> Japanese Pepper Sprout

Nimono, Boiled Food
> Shrimp, Taro and Spinach

Sunomono, Salad
> Cucumbers and Shrimp

Shiizakana, Entrée
> Fried Shrimp (in the shape of chrysanthemum)
>> Grated Radish
>> *Tempura* Sauce

Rice, *Miso* Soup and Pickle
> Rice
> *Miso* Soup with Soy Bean Curd and Green Onion
> Pickled Mustard Greens   *Narazuke*

Bancha, Green Tea

Fruit

Green Tea and Dessert
> *Sencha*
> *Ohagimochi*, Red Bean Paste Coated Rice

HOW TO MAKE SOUP STOCK

I. **Soup Stock from Katsuobushi Dried Bonito Fillet and Konbu Seaweed, Grade I (No. I)**

> $1/3$ oz. *konbu* seaweed
> $1/3$ oz. *katsuobushi* dried bonito fillet
> 4 cups water

Rinse the seaweed slightly. Freshly shave or use packaged shavings of dried bonito fillet.

Boil the water and add the seaweed. Stir the seaweed around several times in the water. Remove the seaweed and continue boiling the hot water. Add the dried bonito fillet and remove the pan from fire immediately. Let stand for 1 minute. Strain and save the material for No. 2 soup stock. The liquid left is No. 1 clear soup stock.

2. **Soup Stock, Grade 2 (No. 2)**

> Use skimmed ingredients from No. 1 soup stock above.

Bring to a boil 2 cups of water into which the strained ingredients from No. 1 have been added. Boil for 8 minutes, remove from fire and skim. This stock is used to cook food.

3. **Soup Stock from Konbu Seaweed and Katsuobushi Dried Bonito Fillet (No. 3)**

> $1/6$ oz. *konbu* seaweed
> $1/6$ oz. *katsuobushi* dried bonito fillet (shaved)
> 4 cups water

Bring the water to a boil with the seaweed and dried bonito fillet in a covered pan. Remove the lid to stir. Keep on boiling for 2–3 minutes. Strain.

Soup stock so obtained is for cooking purposes only (e. g. cooking vegetables).

4. Soup Stock from Dried Shrimp (No. 4)

1¹/₃ ozs. dried small shrimp
2 T. *sake*
4 cups water

Add the shrimp and *sake* to the water. Allow to stand for 10 hours. Boil for 3 minutes and strain.

5. Soup Stock from Dried Young Sardines (No. 5)

1¹/₃ ozs. dried young sardines
2 T. *sake*
4 cups water

Mix the ingredients well and allow to stand for 3 hours. Strain.

6. Soup Stock from Chicken Bones (No. 6)

1 lb. chicken bones
2 small pieces of ginger root
2 green onions
8 cups water

Crush the gingers before boiling. Bring all of the ingredients to a boil over a low heat. Skim the fat and any residue until the soup is clear. Boil down to 4–6 cups of soup. Strain.

7. Soup Stock from Vegetables (No. 7)

8 cups water
2²/₃ ozs. *konbu* seaweed
²/₃ cup soy beans
1¹/₃ ozs. dried gourd
1¹/₃ ozs. dried mushrooms

Wipe the dust from the seaweed with a slightly damp cloth and wash the soy beans and dried mushrooms. Wash the dried gourd by rolling between the palms of the hand under running water. Allow these ingredients to stand for 8 hours in 8 cups of water. Strain and the soup stock is ready for use.

3. To Season Stock for Clear Soup (No. 8)

If one cares to serve clear soup, this is the way to flavor soup stock.

4 cups soup stock (No. 1)
$1\frac{1}{4}$ t. salt
$\frac{1}{3}$ t. soy sauce
monosodium glutamate

Just before boiling, season with salt and soy sauce. Bring the soup stock to boiling point.

CLEAR SOUPS

1. Egg and Greens Soup

      5 eggs
      15 trefoils (greens with 3 leaves)
      5 Japanese pepper sprouts
      4 cups soup stock (No. 8)
      5 sheets of paper (typing size)

Take a piece of paper, fold it in half once, fold it in half once again, open the top to form a cup and break into the cup one egg. Do this with 5 pieces of paper and 5 eggs. This is done to make a "triangle" egg. Put the paper wrapped eggs into boiling water and stand them on the point for 7 minutes. Remove, still wrapped in paper and chill. Remove paper. See figure.

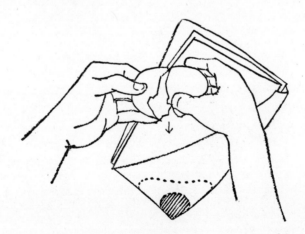

Triangle egg

Into a sheet of paper fold in half twice, make a pocket and drop
an egg to make a "triangle" egg.

Tie 3 stems of trefoil together and trim the stems uniformly. Dip into boiling salted water and then into cold water. Drain. See figure.

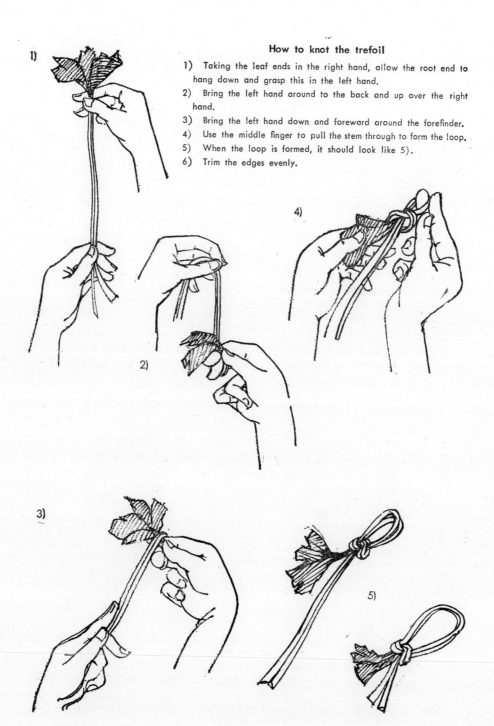

How to knot the trefoil

1) Taking the leaf ends in the right hand, allow the root end to hang down and grasp this in the left hand.
2) Bring the left hand around to the back and up over the right hand.
3) Bring the left hand down and foreward around the forefinder.
4) Use the middle finger to pull the stem through to form the loop.
5) When the loop is formed, it should look like 5).
6) Trim the edges evenly.

15

Prepare the soup bowls, putting into each one, 1 egg, 1 trefoil and 1 Japanese pepper sprout. (A small piece of lemon rind can be substituted for the Japanese pepper sprout.) Cover them with heated soup stock, place the bowl-cover on the bowl and serve.

2. Egg Custard Soup

8 eggs
1/4 lb. spinach
soy sauce
salt
4 cups soup stock (No. 8)
1 1/2 cups soup stock (No. 2)
sugar
monosodium glutamate
yuzu (a kind of grapefruit) or lemon

Beat the eggs well. Add 1 1/2 cups soup stock, 1 1/2 t. soy sauce, 2/3 t. sugar and 2/3 t. monosodium glutamate. Beat again and strain. Pour into a square mold. Steam for 40 minutes over a low flame. Unmold and chill. Divide into equal parts.

Drop washed spinach into boiling salted water and cook. (Be careful not to overcook.) Rinse it in cold water. Drain. Arrange the spinach so that it can be cut into 1 1/2 in. in length pieces.

Place into the soup bowls 1 piece of the egg custard and on the top of that 1 piece of spinach. Pour heated soup carefully over this.

Add a slice or 2 of grapefruit or lemon skin. Cover and serve.

3. Peony Shrimp Soup

10 shrimp (about 1 1/2 in. in size)
15 stalks of bracken (edible fern sprouts)
salt
4 cups soup stock (No. 8)
baking soda
10 toothpicks
Japanese pepper sprouts
cornstarch

Shell (except for the tail) and devein the shrimp. Rinse, drain and

16

Clear Soups

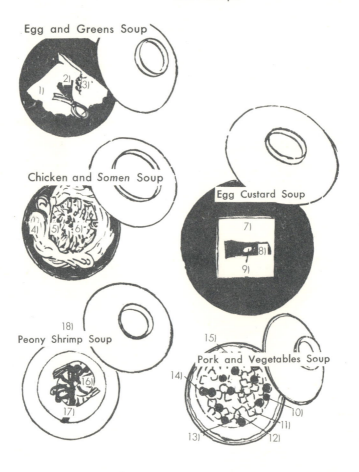

Egg and Greens Soup

Chicken and *Somen* Soup

Egg Custard Soup

Peony Shrimp Soup

Pork and Vegetables Soup

1) egg	3) Japanese pepper sprout
2) trefoil	
4) somen vermicelli	6) Japanese pepper sprout
5) ground ckicken meat	
7) egg and soup stock	9) lemon
8) spinach	
10) green peas	13) carrot
11) pork	14) bamboo shoot
12) dried mushroom	15) potato
16) shrimp	18) Japanese pepper sprout
17) bracken	

salt. Arrange 2 shrimp (see figure) and fasten together at the center with a toothpick. Coat with cornstarch. Drop into boiling water and cook until tender, drain, chill and remove toothpicks carefully.

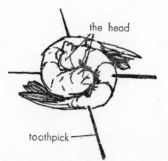

the head

toothpick

Peony shrimp for use clear soup

Taking 2 shrimp, shell and using the head as the center, insert 2 toothpicks as shown.

Put the bracken into a bowl, sprinkle 1/4 t. baking soda over it. Pour into this 1 1/2 cups of hot water. When it is cool, drain off soda water. Put the bracken into hot water and boil about 5 minutes until tender. Drain once more and cut into 2 in. lengths. If canned bracken is used, no cooking is necessary.

Arrange the shrimp and bracken in the soup bowls, cover with the hot soup, add a few Japanese pepper sprouts. Cover with the lids and serve.

4. Chicken and Mushroom Soup

1/2 lb. chicken meat
2–3 *matsutake* mushrooms (about 1 1/2 in. in length)
1 lemon
salt
cornstarch
4 cups soup stock (No. 8)

Discard the skin and slice the chicken into 10 pieces. Salt and allow to stand for 30 minutes. Coat with cornstarch. Drop into boiling salted water and cook till tender. Set aside.

Trim off the ends of the stems of mushrooms and wash. Slice each mushroom into 4 pieces. Boil them for a few minutes over a low flame in the clear soup. Drain, reserving the soup. If using canned mushrooms, no cooking is necessary.

17

Allowing 2 pieces of chicken and 2 slices of mushroom for each soup bowl, add a slice or 2 of lemon skin for flavor. Add heated soup stock, cover with lid and serve.

5. Pork and Vegetable Soup

$1/3$ lb. pork
$1/2$ cup cubed carrots ($1/4$ in.)
1 cup cubed potatoes
$1/2$ cup cubed bamboo shoots*
$11/2$ T. green peas*
4 cups soup stock (No. 3)
a few mushrooms (dried, if possible)

Cube the meat into $1/4$ in. cubes and boil till tender. Drain. Cook the carrots and potatoes till tender. Drain. Cook mushrooms till tender. Drain. (If using dried mushrooms, soak for a few minutes in water just before boiling.) Cook the green peas till tender. Drain.

After cooking, mix together and chill. Divide into soup bowls equally and cover with chilled soup stock. Cover with lid and serve cold.

6. Chicken and Somen (Vermicelli) Soup

$21/2$ ozs. *somen* vermicelli
$1/2$ lb. minced chicken meat
1 T. minced green onion
1 T. minced dried mushroom
$1/2$ egg
$1/3$ t. salt
1 t. soy sauce
$1/2$ t. sugar
monosodium glutamate
4 cups soup stock (No. 7)
Japanese pepper sprouts

Drop the vermicelli into boiling salted water. When tender, rinse in cold water to cool. Drain.

Mix the chicken, green onion, dried mushroom, egg, salt, soy sauce, sugar and monosodium glutamate well and form 5 patties of this mixture. Steam until done thoroughly.

18

Into each soup bowl, place 1 chicken patty and the vermicelli. Add the hot soup stock, cover with the lid and serve.

7. Zoni, Rice Cake Soup

1/2 lb. chicken meat
1/3 *kamaboko* fish cake
1/2 cup bamboo shoots*
15 trefoils or green leaves
10 rice cakes
4 cups soup stock (No. 1)

Slice chicken thin and season slightly with salt.

Cut the fish cake lengthwise into half. Slice into 1/8 in. thick pieces. Cut bamboo shoots diagonally across and then lengthwise, into 4–6 pieces. They can be spread out to form a fan shape.

Tie 3 trefoil stems into a knot (see page 15). Dip quickly into boiling water and then into cold water. Drain, make 5 trefoil knots. Broil the rice cakes without browning. Warm the fish cake and bamboo shoots in a cup of soup stock.

Into each soup bowl, place 2 rice cakes, a bamboo shoot "fan", fish cake, chicken and 1 trefoil, pour in heated soup stock, cover with lid and serve.

SUMASHI-JIRU, STEWS

1. Soboro-jiru, Pork and Vegetable Stew

$^1/_4$ lb. pork
1 small bamboo shoot*
1 green onion
a few dried mushrooms
1 cup bean sprouts
a few string beans
4 cups pork or chicken soup stock
salt
monosodium glutamate

Cut the meat into 2 in. slices and salt. Shred the green onion, bamboo shoot and dried mushrooms (softened in cold water) $1^1/_2$ in. long. Remove the root from the bean sprouts. String the beans and cut into fine strips. Bring the soup stock to a boil. Add all the ingredients except the green onion and boil again. Add 1 t. salt and monosodium glutamate. Skim any residue that forms while boiling. Add the green onion and remove from fire. Serve.

2. Nihei-jiru, Yamaimo and Soy Bean Curd Stew

1 square of soy bean curd
$^3/_4$ lb. *yamaimo* (Japanese yam)
$1^1/_2$ sheets of *nori* seaweed
5 T. radish juice ($^3/_4$ lb. *daikon* radish)
4 cups soup stock (No. 3)
salt
soy sauce
monosodium glutamate

Season the soup stock with 1 $^1/_2$ t. salt, 2 t . soy sauce and a little monosodium glutamate. Heat to boiling. Add cubed (2 in.) soy bean curd. By grating, obtain juice from the radish. Grate the peeled *yamaimo* in an earthen ware mortar (a blender will do nicely). Add the radish juice gradually. Season with 1/2 t. salt and a pinch of monosodium glutamate.

Divide the soup stock into 5 soup bowls, add the *yamaimo* mixture to each, sprinkle with crushed *nori* seaweed and serve.

Before eating, this soup should be stirred once more at the table.

3. Wakame Seaweed Soup

1/2 oz. dried *wakame* seaweed
1 small bamboo shoot*
2/3 oz. dried white bait fish (lancelet)
5 pickled plums
4 cups soup stock (No. 5)
soy sauce
salt
monosodium glutamate

Soften the seaweed in cold water and cut in pieces about 1/2 in. square. Slice the bamboo shoot thinly. Boil the soup stock with the dried white bait fish and bamboo shoot. Season with 11/2 t. salt, 2 t. soy sauce and monosodium glutamate. Add the seaweed and reheat.

To serve, place 1 pickled plum into the soup bowls. Divide the bamboo shoot equally and add the soup stock.

4. Egg and Cabbage Soup

3 eggs
1/3 lb. tender cabbage
4 cups soup stock (No. 5)
salt
soy sauce
monosodium glutamate

Shred the cabbage as fine as possible. Beat the eggs with 1/2 t. salt and a little monosodium glutamate. Season the soup stock with 11/2 t. salt, 2 t. soy sauce and a little monosodium glutamate. Add the cabbage and bring to a boil.

Pour the eggs into the soup through a ladle in which there are

21

holes. Remove the pan from the stove as soon as it comes to a boil. Pour into soup bowls, cover with a lid and serve.

5. Kenchin-jiru, Vegetable Stew

2/3 lb. radish
1/3 lb. carrot
a few dried mushrooms
1 green onion
1 square of soy bean curd
1 T. sesame oil
4 cups soup stock (No. 3)
salt
soy sauce
monosodium glutamate

Remove the water from the soy bean curd by squeezing in a cheesecloth. Chop the radish and carrots into narrow strips (1^1/4 × ^{1}/4 in.). Soften the dried mushrooms in cold water and slice as thin as possible. Cut the green onion into 1^1/2 in. in length pieces and then slice these lengthwise as fine as possible. Saute the carrots, radish and dried mushrooms in sesame oil until tender. Mash the soy bean curd with the fingers, add to the sauted mixture and saute once more. Add the soup stock and season with 2 t. salt and monosodium glutamate.

When this is hot and all the ingredients are tender, add the green onion and without further cooking remove from fire.

Serve immediately.

6. Soy Bean Curd Soup

1 square of soy bean curd
1/4 lb. *matsutake* mushrooms
4 cups soup stock (No. 4)
10 small green onions
salt, soy sauce
monosodium glutamate

Cut the soy bean curd into 2 in. squares. Trim the end of the stem and slice the mushrooms thinly. Season the soup stock with 2 t. salt, 2 t.

soy sauce and monosodium glutamate. Add the soy bean curd and mushrooms and reheat. Do not boil.

Pour into soup bowls, add a pinch of raw minced green onion, cover with the lid and serve.

7. White Fish Chowder

1/3 lb. white fish fillet
1 egg white
5 cups soup stock (No. 1)
leaves of a green vegetable
soy sauce
salt
monosodium glutamate

Pulverize the fish in an earthen ware mortar (a blender can be used). Add the egg white when the fish is nearly powdered. Add 2/3 cup of soup stock. Season with 1/2 t. salt and a pinch of monosodium glutamate. Bring to a boil the remaining soup stock. Add 1 t. soy sauce, 1 t. salt and monosodium glutamate. Add the fish mixture while stirring. Add the green minced leaves and boil for 1 minute.

Serve in covered soup bowls.

8. Noppei-jiru

1/2 lb. chicken (breast meat)
1 *chikuwa* (a roll about 5–6 in. long, 1 in. diameter, made of fish fillet)
1 square of *konnyaku* (a tuberous root)
2/3 lb. radish
1/3 lb. carrots
10 ozs. taro*

1/3 lb. burdock root*
1/3 oz. dried mushrooms
cornstarch
25 gingko nuts or 2 T. green peas*
4 cups soup stock (No. 6)
1 1/2 T. salad oil
salt

23

soy sauce
sugar
monosodium glutamate

Peel and cube (1/4 in.) the radish, carrots, taro and burdock root. Cook the taro and burdock root in boiling salted water until tender. Rinse in cold water and drain. Cube the *konnyaku* and starting in cold water, boil for 10 minutes. Soften the dried mushrooms and chop into same size. Shell the gingko nuts and boil to soften the outer layer of the nutmeat which must be removed. Slice the fish cake diagonally. Into a heated skillet put 2 T. salad oil and add the burdock root, radish, carrots, *konnyaku* and dried mushrooms to saute. Add the chicken and continue to saute. Add the taro, fish cake and nuts with the soup stock. When it boils, season with 1 t. salt, $1\frac{1}{2}$ T. soy sauce, 1 T. sugar and monosodium glutamate. Simmer for 20 minutes. Add the dissolved (in cold water) cornstarch to thicken.

Serve in covered soup bowls.

9. Chawan-mushi, Egg Custard Soup

1/4 lb. chicken meat
1/2 *kamaboko* fish cake
15 trefoils or green leaves
a few mushrooms (dried)
10 small shrimp
15 gingko nuts
2 small tiger lily bulbs (like onion)
2 large eggs
$3\frac{1}{2}$ cups soup stock (No. 1 or 3)
1 lemon
salt
soy sauce
monosodium glutamate

After heating and seasoning the soup stock with 1 t. salt, 1/2 T. soy sauce and monosodium glutamate, allow to cool. Beat the eggs and add the cooled soup stock. Strain. Allow the chicken to stand for 20 minutes in 1/2 T. soy sauce. Cut the fish cake lengthwise and then slice thinly. Prepare the trefoils as figured on page 15. Dip in and out of hot water quickly. Trim the ends of the knot. Soften the dried mushrooms

24

in cold water and trim the stems. Shell and devein the shrimp. Salt slightly. Shell the nuts and boil the nutmeats to remove the outer layer. Remove the outer layer of the tiger lily bulbs and bring the bulbs themselves to a boil in a solution of 2 cups of water and 1 T. vinegar to remove the acrid taste.

Divide the ingredients equally into 5 custard cups, putting the trefoil on the top. Add a small lemon slice. Fill the cups with the egg mixture. These cups usually have lids and are made of china.

The covers should be placed on the cups and set into a steamer, to be steamed for about 20 minutes or until set (test with a silver knife). Serve the cups with the lid on. Very often a piece of paper is folded in half twice and the cup is served on this.

MISO SOUPS

Miso is a soy bean paste made in several varieties, brown *miso*, white *miso*, *chu-miso*, wheat *miso* and others. The soup stock generally used for breakfast soups is prepared from *katsuobushi* dried bonito fillet and usually vegetables are added, however, other foods such as soy bean curd, raw or fried clams, some kinds of seaweed and shellfish are sometimes added. At the evening meal, a more hearty protein soup is desired using pork, chicken, fish, shrimp, crab, etc.

Ingredients that require long cooking, should be pre-boiled in the soup stock. A small amount of this soup stock is used to dissolve the *miso* paste, then the mixture is returned to the soup stock and brought to a boil. Do not boil, for excess cooking destroys the flavor of *miso*. (Foods which must only be heated through can be sufficiently heated when the *miso* mixture is brought to a boil.)

Breakfast Soups

1. Soup with Cabbage and Fried Soy Bean Curd

5 ozs. *chu-miso* paste
2/3 lb. cabbage
2 squares of fried soy bean curd
4 cups soup stock (No. 5)

Shred the soy bean curd and cabbage. Mix the *miso* paste with a little of the soup stock, add soy bean curd and cabbage to the soup and heat. Serve.

2. Soup with Taro and Radish

5 ozs. *chu-miso* paste
1/2 lb. radish
2/3 lb. taro*
4 cups soup stock (No. 5)

26

Peel the taro and slice crosswise 1/4 in. thick into circular pieces. Peel and cut the radish 1 1/2 in. wide. Add them to the soup stock and cook until tender.

Blend the *miso* in a small amount of soup stock. Add to the soup and bring to a boil. Serve.

3. Soup with Eggplant

> 5 ozs. *chu-miso* paste
> 1/2 lb. eggplant
> 4 cups soup stock (No. 5)

Trim the stems of the eggplant. Cut crosswise into pieces 1/2 in. thick. Soak in cold water to remove acrid taste. Drain and cook in the soup stock.

Blend the *miso* in a small amount of soup stock, add to the soup and bring to a boil. Serve.

4. Soup with Ground Soy Beans and Fried Soy Bean Curd

> 5 ozs. *chu-miso* paste
> 2 squares of fried soy bean curd
> 3 T. dried soy beans
> 3 small green onions
> 4 cups soup stock (No. 3)
> 1/6 oz. *katsuobushi* dried bonito fillet

Soak the soy beans overnight to soften in 1 cup water. Grind the soy beans. In the water in which the soy beans were soaked, add the *miso* and the ground soy beans. Bring to a boil, add the strips of the fried soy bean curd and take off fire.

To serve, place a few flakes of dried bonito fillet in the soup bowl, add the soup and garnish with minced green onion. Serve at once.

5. Soup with Turnip

> 5 ozs. *chu-miso* paste
> 3/4 lb. turnip (including leaves)
> 4 cups soup stock (No. 5)

27

Peel and quarter the turnip. Slice each quarter into 1/4 in. slices. Cut the leaves into 4/5 in. lengths. Bring the soup stock to a boil, add the turnip and the leaves, then cook until tender.

Blend the *miso* in a little soup stock and add to the soup. Bring to a boil and serve.

Evening Meal Soups

I. Satsuma-jiru, Soup with Chicken and Vegetables

> 3/4 lb. chopped chicken
> 3/4 lb. taro*
> 1/3 lb. carrots
> 1/2 lb. radish
> a few dried mushrooms
> 5 ozs. *chu-miso* paste
> 6 cups water
> crushed Japanese pepper
> 1 green onion

Bring to a boil 6 cups of cold water and drop the chicken in, simmer about 50 minutes until very tender and skin and bones can be separated easily. Peel and cube (1/2 in.) the taro, carrots and radish. Soften the dried mushrooms in cold water and cut into pieces. Add the vegetables to the chicken and continue boiling until all are tender. Using a little of the broth, dissolve the *miso* and add to the soup. Bring to a boil, add the minced green onion and serve immediately. Sprinkle the crushed Japanese pepper.

2. Soup with Pork and Spinach

> 1/2 lb. pork shoulder
> 1 lb. spinach
> 1 green onion
> 5 ozs. *chu-miso* paste
> 4 cups water
> 2/3 oz. ginger

Blend the *miso* in the water. Add the spinach cut in 1 in. lengths.

28

Bring to a boil. Cube the meat (2 in. cube). Cook in the soup until well done. Remove from fire. Add the minced green onion and grated ginger. Serve immediately.

3. Soup with Amazake (Sweet Wine) and Soy Bean Curd

       5 ozs. *chu-miso* paste
       3 cups soup stock (No. 3)
       1 cup *amazake* (sweet wine)
       1 square of soy bean curd
       3 small green onions

Mix well the *miso* and *amazake* and add the soup stock. Bring to a boil. Crush the soy bean curd with the hands and add to the soup. Bring to a boil once more and remove from fire. Add the minced green onions. Serve immediately.

HORS D'OEUVRES

I. Sweet Pickled Shrimp

10 good sized shrimp
1 small ginger (1$^1/_2$ ozs.)
1 t. poppy seeds or sesame seeds
2 T. vinegar
1$^1/_2$ t. sugar
2$^1/_2$ T. soy sauce
$^2/_3$ t. salt
monosodium glutamate

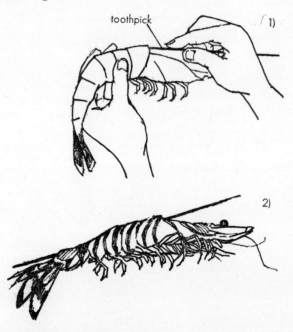

How to insert a toothpick into the shrimp

1) Starting at the head end, insert the toothpick between the shell and the meat of the shrimp before boiling to retain shape.
2) This is the way the shrimp should look after the toothpick has been inserted.

Hors d'Oeuvres

1)	sweet boiled bean	6)	maple leaf
2)	sesame seed	7)	*matsutake* mushroom
3)	shrimp	8)	salmon roe
4)	ginger	9)	chestnut
5)	chicken meat	10)	string bean

Devein the shrimp and using a toothpick insert in the back to keep the shrimp straight. Boil in salted water until tender. (See figure.) Chill. Shell the shrimp and remove the toothpick. Mix the vinegar, salt, sugar and a pinch of monosodium glutamate together. Marinate the shrimp in this sauce.

Peel and mince the ginger. Add the soy sauce and monosodium glutamate and cook together over a low flame stirring constantly, until the soy sauce has been absorbed or evaporated.

To serve, place the marinated shrimp which have been cut into chunks about 3/4 in. in length on a dish. On the top of this place minced ginger and sprinkle a few poppy seeds on the ginger.

2. Broiled Matsutake Mushrooms

5 small sized *matsutake* mushrooms
2 T. *mirin* (a sweet rice wine)
1¹/₂ T. soy sauce
maple leaves

Slice each mushroom into 3 pieces (through the stem and top). Marinate for 1 hour in the soy sauce and *mirin*.

Broil on a wire net over an open fire. Baste once or twice during broiling with the soy sauce and *mirin* mixture.

To serve, place on a small dish with a maple leaf for garnish.

3. Spiced Chicken

1/2 lb. chicken meat
1/2 t. salt
1¹/₂ T. vinegar
1 t. sugar
1/2 t. mustard
monosodium glutamate
sake

Remove the skin of the chicken and rub the meat with salt.
Sprinkle this with *sake*. Steam the chicken until tender and chill. Break into small pieces with the fingers. Dip them into a mixture of the salt, vinegar, sugar, mustard and monosodium glutamate.

Serve.

4. String Beans

       1 cup string beans
       $1/2$ t. salt
       $1/2$ t. sugar
       monosodium glutamate

Remove ends and string from the beans. Drop into boiling salted water (2 t. salt to 5 cups of water). Be careful not to overcook or the green color will fade. Mix salt, sugar and monosodium glutamate and season the drained string beans with this mixture.
       Cut the string beans evenly to serve.

5. Salmon Roe

Use the seasoned salmon roe which is available on the market.
       Serve it as it is.

6. Sweet Boiled Chestnuts

       15 chestnuts (canned)

Use this as it is and serve.

7. Sweet Boiled Beans

       15 sweet boiled beans (canned)
Use this as it is and serve.

       * 5, 6, 7 are exported from Japan to America and are available at certain stores.

SASHIMI, RAW FISH

I. Spring Fish Festival (serves 12 people)

2/3 lb. sea bream
2/3 lb. fresh tuna fish fillet
3 1/3 lbs. cuttlefish
12 cockles
6 snipe fish
3 sheets of *nori* seaweed
2 eggs
1 lb. radish, shredded
1/2 lb. *udo* spikenard
15 *bofu* leaves (a kind of parsnip)
2/3 lb. lotus root
2 cucumbers
1 oz. *metade* knotweed
2 horseradishes, *wasabi* or powdered horseradish
2 *kanten* agar-agar
1 cherry tree twig
1 willow tree twig
10 yellow flowers (spring)
20 cat tails
1 stiff leaf that can be cut
vinegar, salt, sugar, soy sauce, monosodium glutamate

Remove the bones of the sea bream with tweezers. Place the bread board at a slant in the sink, put the sea bream on it covered with a cloth (cheesecloth) and to kill bacteria pour a little boiling water over this (do not cook fish). Quickly remove cloth, plunge the sea bream into cold water and wipe dry. Slice slantingly 1/3 in. thick.

Cut the tuna fish into pieces 1 1/2 × 2/5 in. Putting 3 together, wrap with a band of seaweed.

After preparing the cuttlefish (see page 72), cut the body into 2 equal pieces and placing a slightly smaller piece of seaweed on the

33

top, roll each side of the cuttlefish to make 2 rolls and slice into 1/3 in. slices.

Prepare the cuttlefish as above. Cut the body into 1 × 1 1/2 in. squares and dress with grated hard boiled egg yolk.

Remove the cockle from the shell if it is raw, salt and wash. Cut one side so as to form many "legs".

Scale and remove the entrails from the snipe fish. Cut into 3 pieces and slice into strips.

Cut the radish into 2 in. lengths, peel and cut around (as though peeling), spread out on a board and cut into strips across the grain. Soak in cold water and drain.

Cut the spikenard as figured.

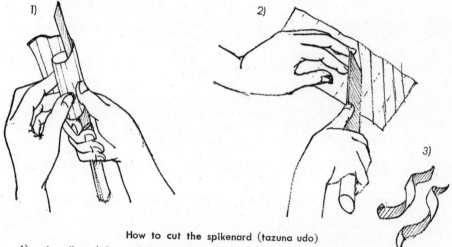

How to cut the spikenard (tazuna udo)

1) *udo* spikenard is cut into 2 in. lengths and peeled as thinly as possible.

2) After peeling, lay the peelings flat and cut into diagonal strips so that the end result is as 3).

Wash the *bofu* leaves and soak in cold water. Drain.

Cut the cucumbers as the radish is cut.

Wash *metade* and drain.

If using the powdered horseradish dissolve in water or use grated fresh horseradish root.

Soften the *kanten* in cold water and squeeze. Tear apart with fingers and add to 4 cups water (2 cups water per 1 *kanten*). Heat and when the *kanten* melts, add 1/8 t. salt, 2 t. sugar and monosodium

34

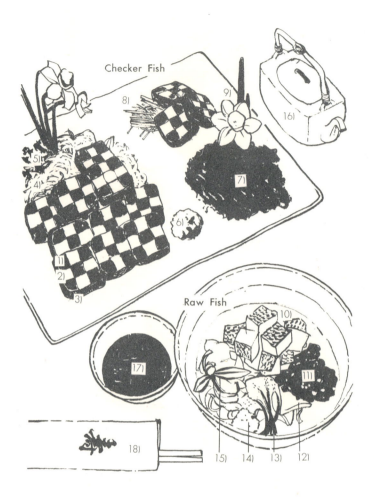

1) tuna fish	6) horseradish or *wasabi*
2) flounder	7) *ugu*
3) *nori* seaweed	8) cucumber
4) radish	9) daffodil
5) *metade* smartweed	

10) cubed sea bream	15) orchid
11) *nori* seaweed	
12) cuttlefish	16) soy sauce pitcher
13) string bean	17) soy sauce
14) horseradish or *wasabi*	18) chopsticks

glutamate. Skim the residue which rises. Set to mold in an oblong pan, so that it can be cut into strips when solidified.

Peel the lotus root and place in vinegar water to prevent discoloration. Boil in a new solution of vinegar and water until tender. Cut as shown (page 40). Since they are supposed to represent baskets, place a pebble or two in one.

Cut the stiff leaves to form "mountains". Follow the picture to arrange the ingredients. A dark dish that lends color to the "river" is best.

The dish as arranged in the picture suggests spring in Japan. Trees, mountains, spring flowers, stones near the river, etc. Serve the dish and individual dishes with a spoonful of horseradish and a side dish of soy sauce. This is one of the most typical of Japanese foods.

2. Checker Fish

1/2 lb. tuna fish fillet
1/2 lb. flounder fillet
1 sheet of *nori* seaweed
2/3 lb. radish
2 ozs. *ugu*
2/3 oz. *metade* knotweed
a little horseradish or *wasabi*
daffodil flowers
soy sauce

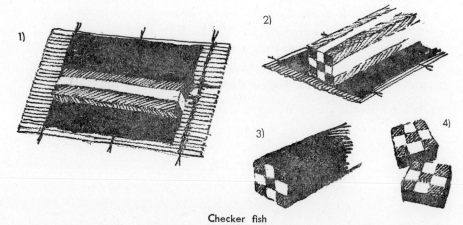

Checker fish

1)–4) On a bamboo mat place a sheet of seaweed, on the top place white and pink fish fillets strips alternately. Wrap the seaweed around the 9 strips of fish and slice.

35

Cut the tuna fish and flounder into squares $1/4 \times 8$ in. Place the sea-weed on a bamboo mat and as the figure, place the strips of fish and wrap with the seaweed. Slice. Wash and drain *metade*. Use either powdered or fresh horseradish. Wash, dip *ugu* in the salted hot water and drain after wash with running water. Make a "stand" of a round of radish for each daffodil flower to stand in.

Serve the slices of checker board fish with a few *metade* and a spoonful of horseradish, with a side dish of soy sauce and a daffodil in a suitable spot to make it appear beautiful.

3. Sea Bream and Cuttlefish

1 small sea bream
1 ($1^1/_3$ lbs.) cuttlefish
3 young string beans
2 sheets of *nori* seaweed
a little horseradish or *wasabi*
soy sauce
1 t. poppy seeds or minced white seasame seeds.

See page 33 for preparing this sea bream. Cut the sea bream into cubes ($3/_4$ in.). Cut the cuttlefish, after preparing as on page 72, into squares $1 \times 1^1/_2$ in. and cut on one side every $1/4$ in. to make "legs". Very quickly dip in and out of boiling water and drain. Boil the string beans until tender (keep the green color), slice into $1/_2$ lengthwise and then slantwise in $1^1/_2$ in. long strips. Dip 1 end into the ground poppy seeds to look like a rice plant. Make a ball of 1 sheet of seaweed in the hand, dip quickly in and out of water and squeeze.

Divide the ingredients into 5 equal portions with a little horseradish and put on individual dishes. Serve with a small dish of soy sauce.

KUCHITORI, SPECIAL OCCASION SIDE DISHES

I. Tidbit Platter

a. Tazuna Zushi, Fish and Egg Squares

    10 shrimp
    6 sillagoes
    14 eggs
    salt
    vinegar
    sugar
    monosodium glutamate

Devein the shrimp, insert skewers and cook in boiling salted water until tender. When cool, shell. Cut into half lengthwise. Mix 3 T. vinegar, 1 1/2 t. salt, 1 T. sugar and monosodium glutamate. Marinate the shrimp until ready to use.

Split the sillagoes into half and remove the bones. Salt and allow to stand for 1 hour. Rinse, drain and add 3 T. vinegar. Let stand until the skin can be removed easily and peel.

Beat 14 eggs, add 1 1/2 t. salt, 2 T. sugar and monosodium glutamate

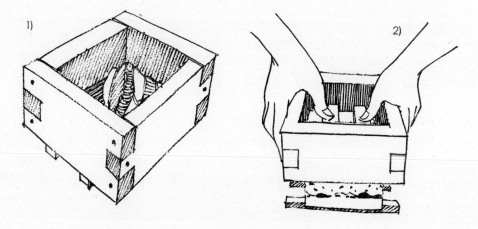

37

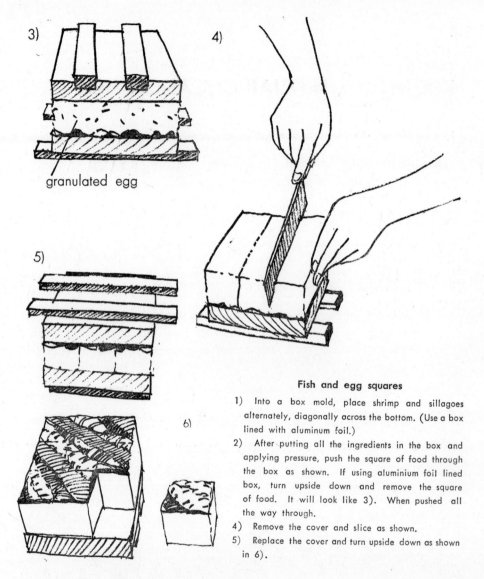

3)

granulated egg

5)

4)

6)

Fish and egg squares

1) Into a box mold, place shrimp and sillagoes alternately, diagonally across the bottom. (Use a box lined with aluminum foil.)

2) After putting all the ingredients in the box and applying pressure, push the square of food through the box as shown. If using aluminium foil lined box, turn upside down and remove the square of food. It will look like 3). When pushed all the way through.

3) Remove the cover and slice as shown.

4) Replace the cover and turn upside down as shown in 6).

and mix well. Fry while stirring continuously. When done, press through a sieve or food mill while hot. When cooled, add 4 T. vinegar and monosodium glutamate. Mix well.

Place the shrimp, outside down, in the bottom of a square mold (*oshiwaku*) diagonally and alternately with sillagoes. On the top of the fish put $1/2$ of the egg. Press to mold and place a weight on the top

Tazuna Zushi

Urauchi Shiitake

Gizeidofu, Steamed Soy Bean Curd Roll

Roast Chicken

Jakago Renkon, Lotus Root

Molded Kanten

1) snipe fish
2) shrimp

3) Japanese pepper sprout

4) dried mushroom

5) shrimp paste

6) soy bean curd
carrot, dried mishroom

7) chicken meat
8) lemon

9) chicken meat
10) *haran*

11) lotus root

12) cherry flower shaped *kanten*
13) *kanten*
sugar

15) Japanese pepper sprout
16) red pepper

14) *kanten* shaped gourd

for about 10 minutes. Remove from the mold. Make 2. Cut to the correct size to fit the plate on which it is to be served.

b. Urauchi Shiitake, Filled Mushrooms

> 30 dried mushrooms
> 2/3 lb. shrimp
> 1 cup soup stock (No. 2 or 3)
> 1 egg white
> soy sauce
> sugar
> salt
> cornstarch
> monosodium glutamate

Soften the dried mushrooms in cold water and remove the stems. Mix 1 cup soup stock, 1 1/2 T. soy sauce and 1 T. sugar and bring to a boil. Add the dried mushrooms and cook until well flavored. Remove from fire and drain.

Devein, shell and grind the shrimp. Add 1 egg white, 1 t. cornstarch, 1 t. salt and monosodium glutamate. Mix well to make shrimp paste. Squeeze lightly, coat the underside of the dried mushroom cap lightly with cornstarch and fill the underside with shrimp paste. Steam until the shrimp is done.

c. Gizeidofu, Steamed Soy Bean Curd Roll

> 3 squares of soy bean curd
> 2 ozs. carrots
> 10 small dried mushrooms
> 2 eggs
> salt
> sugar
> monosodium glutamate

In a cheesecloth, squeeze the liquid from the soy bean curd. Mince and boil the carrots. Soften the dried mushrooms in cold water and mince.

Mash the soy bean curd and add the carrots, dried mushrooms, eggs, 1 t. salt, 2 1/3 t. sugar and monosodium glutamate. Mix well. In a well wrung damp cloth, wrap 1/2 of the mixture and make a roll 1 1/2 in. in diameter. Tie each end with thread. Make 2. Steam for 25 minutes. Cool and remove from cloth and slice 1/3 in. thick.

d. Jakago Renkon, Lotus Roots

> $2/3$ lb. lotus roots
> vinegar
> salt
> sugar
> monosodium glutamate

Peel the lotus roots and place in vinegar water to prevent discoloration. Cut into half lengthwise and slice $2/3$ in. thick. Boil in a new solution of vinegar and water until tender.   Cut as shown in the figure.

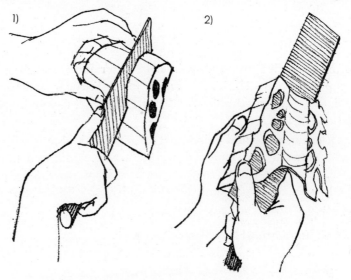

How to make jakago renkon

1) After cutting the lotus root into half lengthwise, cut diagonally as shown.
2) After rounding the corners, peel each small section, without breaking into pieces as far toward the center as possible. (Much as an apple would be peeled.)

Mix 4 T. vinegar, $1/2$ t. salt, 1 T. sugar and monosodium glutamate well, marinate the lotus roots into above sauce.

e. Roast Chicken

> 1 lb. chicken meat
> 1 lemon
> *mirin*
> salad oil
> soy sauce

Kuchitori, Special Occasion Side Dishes

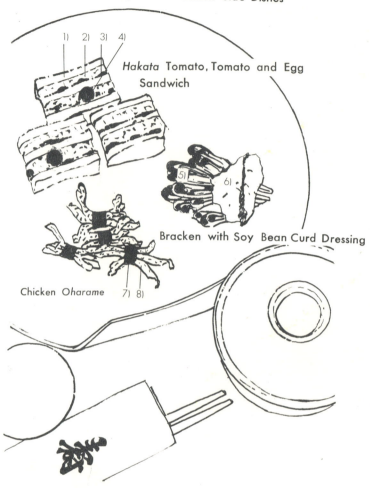

Hakata Tomato, Tomato and Egg
Sandwich

Bracken with Soy Bean Curd Dressing

Chicken Oharame

1)	bread	3)	tomato
2)	egg	4)	green peas
5)	bracken	6)	soy bean curd dressing
7)	nori seaweed	8)	chicken meat

To prepare this, see page 48.

f. Molded Kanten

> 3 *kanten* agar-agar
> 6 cups water
> 2/3 lb. sugar
> red and green coloring

Soften the *kanten* in cold water and squeeze. Tear apart with fingers and add to 6 cups water. Heat and when the *kanten* melts, add the sugar. Skim and boil until only 1/2 of the mixture is left. Divide in half and add red to one half, green to the other, strain, pour each into a 6 in. square cake pan and cool. Cut the red *kanten* into flower shapes and the green into a pretty shape with a cookie cutter.

When all 6 tidbits are prepared, arrange as shown in the picture (opposite page 38) on a large plate and serve.

The following 4 kinds of side dishes can be served together or separately. If served together, place the *hakata* tomato away from and the chicken *oharame* toward the person eating.

2. Hakata Tomato, Tomato and Egg Sandwich

(makes 6 servings)

> 6 slices day of old sandwich bread
> 1 (4 ozs.) tomato
> 2 eggs
> 1 T. green peas*
> 1½ t. sugar
> 1/3 t. salt
> monosodium glutamate

Peel the tomato and slice 1/4 in. thick. Beat 2 eggs and add 1/3 t. salt, 1½ t. sugar and monosodium glutamate. Mix well. Fry while stirring constantly. (It should be the consistency of paste when done.) Remove from fire and add the green peas.

Divide the egg and tomato to make 2 triple deck sandwiches. Placing the tomato on the top of the egg between 2 slices of bread. Add more egg and tomato and 1 more slice of bread. Wrap in a

41

damp cloth and place under a heavy object. Cut off edges and make 6 smaller slices of sandwich.

3. Chicken Oharame

 $1/3$ lb. chicken meat
 $1/2$ sheet of *nori* seaweed
 $1/2$ egg white
 1 T. soy sauce
 1 T. *sake*
 salad oil

Remove the skin from the chicken and cut in strips $2 \times 1/5$ in. Allow to stand for about 1 hour in the soy sauce and *sake*.

Cut across the width of the seaweed, to make strips, $1/2$ in. in width. Taking 4–5 strips of chicken in one hand, with the other hand dip one side of the seaweed in and out of egg white and fasten the seaweed around the center of the chicken.

Fry and place on absorbent paper.

4. Bracken with Soy Bean Curd Dressing

 4 ozs. bracken* (if unavailable, use bamboo shoots or mushrooms)
 1 square of soy bean curd
 2 T. white sesame seeds
 $1/2$ t. baking soda
 soy sauce
 salt
 sugar
 monosodium glutamate

To prepare the bracken, see page 17. Cut into $1^{1}/2$ in. lengths. Add $1/2$ T. soy sauce and monosodium glutamate to the bracken and mix well. Drain. Squeeze the liquid from the soy bean curd by placing in cheesecloth. Place the white sesame seeds in an ungreased skillet and heat until they "jump", remove and grind. Add the soy bean curd and mix well. (If it becomes too thick, add a little of soup stock and mix again.) Add $1/2$ t. salt and $1/2$ T. sugar and mix well. Strain. Add the bracken. Mix well.

42

BROILED DISHES

I. Broiled Sea Bream

     5 small sea breams
     1½ ozs. fresh ginger
     1 lemon
     1 small radish
     salt
     soy sauce

Scale, clean, remove entrails and wash fish. Salt on both sides and let stand for 2 hours. Wash quickly and wipe dry. Insert a skewer and fasten a bit of vegetable on the end of the fins as shown on the figure. The fish must be broiled in the form of a living fish with one side,

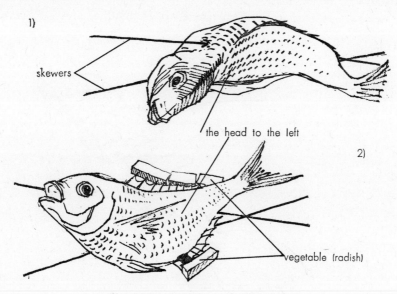

1)

skewers

the head to the left

2)

vegetable (radish)

How to insert skewers into sea bream

1) Insert 1 skewer into the side of the fish through the bones and out again by the tail to curve the fish. Insert the other skewer in a crosswise fashion.
2) Place bits of vegetables on the fins to hold them straight.

43

which is called the "front" which is beautiful, therefore, the other side, called the back is the place for inserting skewers.

Salt and boil the "front" side first, when turning, turn by the skewers. When done, remove the skewers carefully so that the fish is not broken. To serve, garnish with gingers shaped brush, with a side dish of equal parts of lemon juice and soy sauce for dipping the fish.

2. Glazed Broiled Fish (mackerel, yellowfish, etc.)

5 fish fillets
soy sauce
mirin

Allow 1 piece of fish per person. Soak for 2 hours in the soup stock to which has been added 4 T. *mirin* and 3 T. soy sauce. Broil using either skewers as shown or on a wire rack. Baste the fish 2–3 times during broiling by dipping it into the mixture in which it was soaked. Boil 2 T. soy sauce and 3 T. *mirin* until thickened and pour over the fish that has been placed on individual plates. Serve.

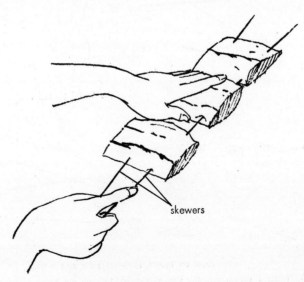

skewers

How to insert skewers into fish fillets
When broiling slices of fish, insert the skewers as figured.

44

3. Broiled White Fish Fillet Garnished with Egg Yolk

> 5 fish fillets
> 1 egg yolk
> salt
> *sake*
> *mirin*
> monosodium glutamate

Salt the fish on both sides and allow to stand for 2 hours. Wash quickly and wipe dry. Cover with 1/3 cup *sake* until ready to broil.

Beat the egg yolk together with 1/2 t. *mirin* and monosodium glutamate.

After inserting skewers as shown on page 44, broil on both sides. After broiling brush the front side only with the egg yolk mixture.

Serve on individual plates, egg yolk side up.

4. Broiled Fish with Miso

> 5 fish
> 4 ozs. brown *miso* paste
> 1/2 T. minced green onion or onion
> 1 1/2 ozs. grated ginger
> oil
> sugar
> monosodium glutamate

Clean and remove the entrails from the fish. On both sides of the fish, cut with a knife like this # so that the flavor can penetrate the skin.

Mix *miso*, 3 t. sugar and monosodium glutamate well. Add the minced green onion. Insert skewers as shown on page 43. After the front side has been broiled and while the other side is broiling, cover the "front" side with *miso* sauce. While covering the underside with *miso* sauce, allow the front side to be broiled again slightly. Turn once more so that the underside can also be broiled slightly again.

Serve on individual plates with a garnish of grated ginger.

5. Miso Cured Fish

> 5 fish fillets

45

1¹/2 lbs. white *miso* paste
salt
sugar
sake
cheesecloth

Salt fish well on both sides and allow to stand for 3 hours.

Add to *miso*, 4 T. each of *sake* and sugar. Mix well.

Into a 3–4 in. deep pan, put a layer of ¹/2 of the *miso* sauce, spread a sheet of cheesecloth, lay the fish flat and spread the cheese-cloth back over the top of the fish. Add the remaining ¹/2 *miso* sauce and allow to remain as is in a cool place for at least 24 hours. Broil and serve.

6. Sea Bream Crown with a Ginger Brush (makes 4 servings)

2 heads of sea bream
4 stalks of fresh ginger
mirin
soy sauce
vinegar

Split the sea bream heads into 2 symmetrical pieces. Add 6 T. *mirin* and 4 T. soy sauce and allow to soak for at least 30 minutes, 1 hour is better.

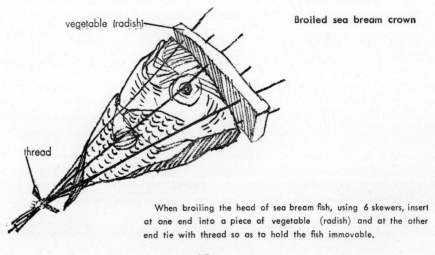

vegetable (radish)

Broiled sea bream crown

thread

When broiling the head of sea bream fish, using 6 skewers, insert at one end into a piece of vegetable (radish) and at the other end tie with thread so as to hold the fish immovable.

46

Bamboo Shoot and Eel Sandwich

Sea Bream Crown with a Ginger Brush

Broiled Chicken

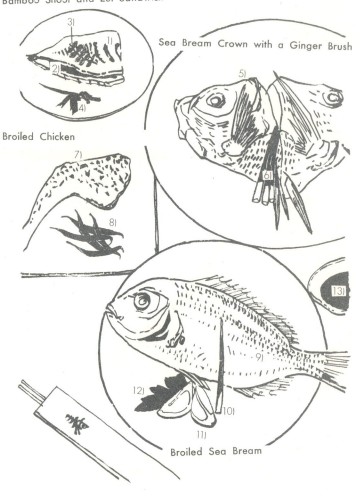

Broiled Sea Bream

1)	bamboo shoot	3)	Japanese pepper sprout
2)	broiled eel	4)	orchid
5)	head of sea bream	6)	fresh ginger shaped brush
7)	chicken meat	8)	string bean
9)	sea bream	12)	chrysanthemum leaf
10)	fresh ginger shaped brush		
11)	lemon	13)	lemon, vinegar and soy sauce

Insert the skewers as shown in the figure on page 46. Place a piece of vegetable on the end of the fins to keep the fins in a natural position. Broil the front side first and turn, basting 2–3 times with the sauce. Boil the brush shaped ginger in vinegar a few minutes, rinse quickly in cold water and place in a solution of equal parts of vinegar and water.

Serve on individual plates, 1 fish per person, garnished with 1 ginger shaped brush.

7. Broiled Salted Shrimp

10 shrimp
1 t. black sesame seeds
1 lemon
salt
soy sauce

Split the shrimp lengthwise (but do not completely divide) with the shell on and devein. Lay flat and on the inside sprinkle salt and black sesame seeds. Broil the seasoned side first and turn.

Serve on individual plates, with a side dish of equal parts of lemon juice and soy sauce.

8. Broiled Chicken

5 chicken legs
1 T. white sesame seeds
1/2 green onion or onion, minced
2–3 small red pepper, minced
soy sauce
mirin
salad oil

Mix well 4 T. soy sauce, 6 T. *mirin*, parched sesame seeds, minced red pepper and minced green onion. Into this mixture add the chicken legs and marinate for 2 hours.

Fry in a heated skillet which salad oil has been added. While frying, baste 2–3 times with the sauce. Serve on individual plates with a knife and fork.

47

9. Broiled Chicken and Mushrooms

1/2 lb. ground chicken meat
2 dried mushrooms
2/3 oz. bamboo shoots*
4 in. small green onion or onion, minced
1 egg
1 t. poppy seeds or sesame seeds
soy sauce
sake
salt
sugar
monosodium glutamate

Soak the dried mushrooms in cold water until soft. Mince the dried mushrooms, bamboo shoots and green onions.

To the minced vegetables add the ground chicken meat, 1 T. soy sauce, 1/2 T. *sake*, 1/2 t. salt, 1/2 T. sugar, 1 egg and monosodium glutamate. Mix well and form 1 large square 3/4 in. thick. Spread on a cookie sheet. Sprinkle this with poppy seeds and bake in the oven until the chicken is tender. Allow to cool. Cut into 10 squares allowing 2 squares per person and serve on individual plates.

10. Roast Chicken

10 ozs. chicken meat
1 lemon
salad oil
soy sauce
mirin

Allow the chicken which has been cut into 1/4 in. slices, to soak in a mixture of 2 T. soy sauce and 3 T. *mirin* for 1 hour.

Into a heated skillet, add 1 T. salad oil and fry the chicken twice dipping into the mixture of soy sauce and *mirin* and fry again.

Serve in the form of sandwiches, allowing 2 lemon slices to 1 chicken slice.

11. Bamboo Shoot and Eel Sandwich

21/2 bamboo shoots* of about 4 in. length

5 pieces of broiled eel* of about 3 in. length (1 live-eel)
mirin
sake
soy sauce
sugar
crushed Japanese pepper
white karo syrup
5 Japanese pepper sprouts

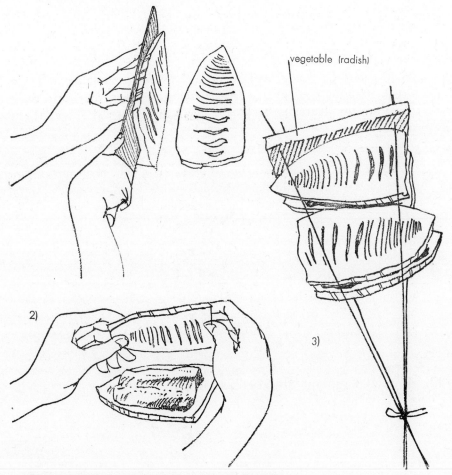

vegetable (radish)

2)

3)

How to make the bamboo shoot and eel sandwich

1) Cut the bamboo shoots as figured.
2) Between 2 slices of bamboo shoots, place 1 slice of eel.
3) Using 4 skewers, insert 1 end into a piece of vegetable (radish). Tie the other end with thread to make the "sandwiches" immovable and broil.

Cut 4 bamboo shoots slices 4 in. long and ¹/₃ in. thick. Pour 3 T. *mirin* and 2 T. soy sauce over the bamboo shoots and allow to soak for 2 hours.

If the eel is prepared from fresh living eels (this is the way they are purchased in Japan) dump the eel and surrounding water into the sink. After the water has drained off, with a piece of paper to prevent slipping, quickly grab the eel by the neck and tail. Placing it on a wooden board, release the tail and quickly stab the eel through the neck with an ice pick, fastening it to the board. Grab the tail and stab with another ice pick just between the tail and body. Quickly slit the eel from pick to pick on the belly side and cut off the head and tail on the outer side of the picks. Remove the entrails and bones and open flat. Cut into 3 in. lengths crosswise and hold over a low flame until the moisture has dried. (If using the eels for *tempura*, at this point they are ready to place in the batter.) Hold the head and bones also over the flame until dry.

Steam the meat for 12 minutes.

Mix 2 T. *mirin*, 2 T. *sake*, 3 T. soy sauce, 2 T. sugar and 1 T. white karo syrup well. Into this add the head and bones and boil until the sauce has evaporated to ¹/₃ of the original volume making "eel gravy".

The steamed meat must be broiled over an open fire while basting frequently with the sauce until browned and tender.

Make "sandwiches" using the bamboo shoots on either side of the fish. Broil both sides 2–3 times over a charcoal fire redipping in the mixture in which the bamboo shoots were soaked. Withdraw skewers. Serve with the "eel gravy" and a sprinkle of crushed Japanese pepper and a Japanese pepper sprout.

12. Broiled Eggplant and Eel Sandwich

2 eggplants
5 pieces of broiled eel* each about 2¹/₂ in. length
mirin
soy sauce
crushed Japanese pepper

Slice the eggplants as in the previous recipe for bamboo sprouts. Place in salt water to prevent discoloration. Between 2 slices insert the eel as in the previous recipe. See page 49.

Mix 2 T. soy sauce and 3 T. *mirin* to use for basting the "sandwiches" during broiling.

Thicken the soup stock and pour over the sandwiches as gravy.

To serve, garnish with crushed Japanese pepper.

BOILED MEAT AND VEGETABLES

I. Boiled Lobsters (makes 3 servings)

> 1^1/$_2$ lbs. fresh lobsters
> 1/3 cup *mirin*
> 1/3 cup *sake*
> 2^1/$_2$ T. soy sauce
> 2 t. sugar

Wash the lobsters and after cutting the head off (do not throw away) cut each segment apart and cut off the tail. Cut the legs off at the first joint. Cut the head lengthwise into symmetrical pieces. Each of the pieces of head should be cut again into 3 sections crosswise.

Mix the *mirin*, *sake*, soy sauce and sugar in a deep sauce pan and bring to a boil. Into this, add the lobsters beginning with the head. Allow the shell side to be against the pan. Continue to add the pieces from the head to the legs in the same manner. Using a cover that will fit inside the pan, put it on so that the cover is resting on the lobster mixture. Boil for a short time (4–5 minutes) over a strong flame. While boiling, if there are any parts not covered by the sauce, turn these pieces over once. While still hot, remove to a plate and pour the remaining sauce over the top.

2. Boiled Chicken and Vegetables

> 1 lb. cut young chicken (with bones)
> 1^1/$_2$ lbs. bamboo shoots*
> 1/3 lb. carrots
> 15 small dried mushrooms
> a few string beans
> 1 t. soy sauce
> 2 t. salt
> monosodium glutamate
> cornstarch
> sugar

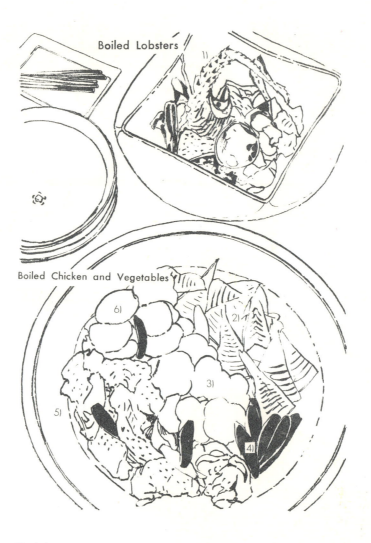

Boiled Lobsters

Boiled Chicken and Vegetables

1) lobster

2) bamboo shoot   5) chicken meat

3) carrot   6) dried mushroom

4) string bean

Have the meat man cut the chicken into chunks about 1 in. square. Into 8 cups of boiling water, drop the washed chicken and boil for 40 minutes over a low flame. Skim several times while boiling. After 40 minutes of boiling, add 2 t. salt and 1 t. soy sauce and continue boiling for 10 minutes.

From the pointed end of the bamboo shoots, cut into cross sections $2^3/_8$ in. in thickness. Cut these sections into quarters. On the thick end, because this is tough, cut the cross sections into $2/_3$ in. thick rounds and use as are.

Slice the carrots into rounds and cut the edges into flower shapes.

Soak the dried mushrooms in cold water until soft and remove the stems. String the beans and cut the ends so that all are the some length. Drop the string beans into salted boiling water and parboil. (Be careful to keep the green color.) Rinse in cold water and drain.

Put the soup stock into a clean large pan. Add the dried mushrooms, carrots and bamboo shoots and boil long enough to flavor. Just before removing from fire, drop in the string beans.

On 5 plates arrange the vegetables and chicken. Thicken the remaining soup with cornstarch. Pour the gravy over the meat and vegetables and serve.

3. Boiled Vegetables

3/4 lb. taro*
2/3 oz. dried mushrooms
2 squares of *nama-age* half-fried soy bean curd
1/2 lb. bamboo shoots*
3 ozs. string beans
1 cup soup stock (No. 2 or 3)
soy sauce
sake
mirin
sugar
salt
monosodium glutamate

Peel and cube (1/2 in. square) the taro. Starting in salted water, boil until tender. Rinse in cold water and allow to cool. Drain. Soften the dried mushrooms in cold water. Mix and boil for a few minutes, $1^1/2$ T. each of soy sauce, *mirin* and *sake* and 2 t. sugar. When this boils, add the dried mushrooms and continue boiling with a cover on until flavored. Drain in a strainer or bamboo basket.

Cube ($1/2$ in.) the bamboo shoots. Cut the half-fried soy bean curd into the same size as the bamboo shoots.

Into a clean pan, put 1 cup of soup stock, 3 T. soy sauce, 2 T. *sake*, 2 T. *mirin* and $1/2$ T. sugar and when it boils, add the half-fried soy bean curd. Boil covered over a very low flame for 15–20 minutes, remove from fire and allow to cool in the pan. Place on a dish without sauce when cool.

Add the sauce from cooking the dried mushrooms to the sauce used to cook the half-fried soy bean curd. Add $1^1/2$ T. each *sake*, *mirin* and soy sauce and when it boils, add the taro and bamboo shoots. Drop the string beans into salted boiling water and parboil. (Be careful not to lose the green color.) Rinse in cold water and allow to cool. Drain. Mix $1/4$ t. salt, $1/2$ t. sugar and monosodium glutamate and add the string beans.

Arrange the taro, bamboo shoots, half-fried soy bean curd, dried mushrooms and string beans on a plate and serve.

4. Pork Stew

$2/3$ lb. pork shoulder, cut into 10 equal pieces
2 lbs. radish
2 green onions
$1/2$ oz. ginger
sake
soy sauce
sugar

Slice the radish into $1^1/3$ in. thick, peel and quarter. Crush the green onions and ginger.

Into a pan, put 4 cups water, 1 T. *sake*, crushed green onions and ginger and bring to a boil. Add the pork and radish. After cooking 1 hour over a low flame, add $2^1/2$ T. soy sauce and $1^1/2$ T. sugar and continue boiling until well flavored.

Serve in soup bowls.

5. Pork and Taro

2/3 lb. pork shoulder (cubed 1 1/4 in.)
1 1/3 lbs. taro*
1 small ginger
1/2 T. salad oil
1 T. *sake*
2 T. soy sauce
1/2 t. salt
1 1/2 T. sugar

Slice the ginger thinly.

Into a skillet heat the salad oil and when hot, add the pork and ginger and brown. Remove the pork into a bamboo basket or a strainer to drain.

Peel the taro, cube into 3/4 in. chunks and boil in salted water. Rinse and drain. Into a saucepan, put the 3 cups water, 1 T. *sake*, 2 T. soy sauce, 1/2 t. salt, 1 1/2 T. sugar, pork and taro and over a low flame, boil covered until the soup is nearly absorbed. Serve.

6. Boiled Ham and Green Peas

1 2/3 lbs. green peas*
1/3 lb. boneless ham, diced to size of a pea
2 cups soup stock (No. 3)
soy sauce
salt
sugar
monosodium glutamate
1 T. cornstarch

Shell the green peas and boil in 2 cups soup stock. When half-done add 1/2 T. soy sauce, 1/2 t. salt and 1/2 T. sugar and boil over a low flame until tender. Add monosodium glutamate. Add the ham to the soup and when the ham is warmed by the soup stock, add the cornstarch which has been dissolved in 2 T. water. Stir until thickened. Serve while hot in soup bowls.

7. Aburage Cabbage Rolls

6 large cabbage leaves

3 sheets of *aburage* fried soy bean curd
1/2 lb. ground pork
a few green onions
3 small dried mushrooms
1/2 egg
1 1/2 cups soup stock (No. 2 or 3)
soy sauce
salt
sake
sugar
monosodium glutamate

Remove the "veins" of the cabbage and dip the tender parts in and out of boiling water quickly. Drain.

Insert a knife into 3 sides of the fried soy bean curd and open it flat. Placing the inside down in a bamboo basket or a strainer, pour hot water over it to remove excess oil. Drain.

To the pork, add the minced :green onions, dried mushrooms, 1/2 T. *sake*, 1/3 t. salt, 1 t. sugar, 1/2 beaten egg and monosodium glutamate and mix well.

On a bread board, spread out 2 cabbage leaves, place on them 1/6 of the pork mixture, 1 piece of fried soy bean curd and again 1/6 of the pork. Roll away from yourself to make a cabbage roll. Wind 1 piece of thread around this to hold form. Make 3.

Mix and boil 1 1/2 cups soup stock, 2 t. soy sauce, 1/2 t. salt, 1/2 T. sugar and monosodium glutamate. Add the cabbage rolls to this, cover and boil until well flavored. During the boiling, occasionally turn the cabbage rolls. Remove the cabbage from the sauce and the threads from the cabbage. Cut into chunks 1 1/3 in. in length. Place on a plate with the cut end up. Pour the sauce over the cabbage and serve.

8. Stuffed Cucumber Stew

15 (4 in.) cucumbers
1/2 lb. ground chicken meat
1 T. minced :green onion
1 1/2 T. white sesame seeds
1 red pepper
cornstarch

salad oil
2^1/2 cups soup stock (No. 6)
soy sauce
salt
sugar
monosodium glutamate

Cut the end part off the cucumbers and insert the knife as shown below. Make 6 slits around 1 cucumber. Saute the cucumbers in salad oil without browning. Mix well the chicken, green onion, parched (heating in skillet until they "jump") white sesame seeds, minced red pepper, 1/2 T. soy sauce, 1/2 t. salt, 1 t. sugar and monosodium glutamate. Insert this mixture into the cucumber slits until the cucumbers bulge, but be sure the meat mixture will not fall out during cooking.

Into boiling 2^1/2 cups soup stock, add 1 t. salt and monosodium glutamate, add all of the cucumbers and cook until the chicken is done. Remove the cucumbers. Into the leftover soup, add the dissolved cornstarch to thicken.

Pour the gravy over the cucumbers and serve.

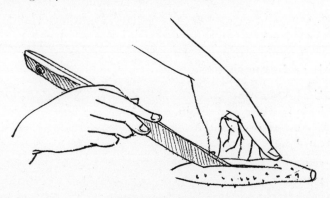

Stuffed cucumber stew
To fill the cucumber before boiling, insert the knife and make an incision way down. Trim the ends.

9. Chicken and Onions

1 lb. onions
1/2 lb. chicken meat
1/2 oz. dried mushrooms

57

3 eggs
1 1/2 cups soup stock (No. 2 or 3)
2 T. green peas*
sugar
salt
soy sauce
monosodium glutamate
crushed Japanese pepper

Cut the onions into half and then slice thin from side to side. Slice the chicken thin. Do not remove the skin. Soak the dried mushrooms in cold water and cut into strips.

Beat eggs with 1/3 t. salt and monosodium glutamate and mix well.

Into the soup stock, add 1 1/2 T. soy sauce, 1 t. salt, 1 T. sugar and monosodium glutamate. Bring to a boil. When the soup stock boils, add onions and continue boiling covered, over a low flame. When the onions are tender, add the chicken and dried mushrooms and cook until the chicken is tender. Pour the eggs into the soup through a ladle in which there are large holes. Sprinkle the green peas on the top of the soup and continue boiling for a few minutes over a low flame. When the egg is coagulated, serve on plates immediately. Sprinkle a small amount of crushed Japanese pepper.

10. Pork and Squash Stew

1 1/3 lbs. squash
1/2 lb. pork, cubed 4/5 in.
2 cups soup stock (No. 2 or 3)
salad oil
salt
pepper
cornstarch
monosodium glutamate

Select a fresh tender skinned squash and cut into 1 1/5 in. cubes.

Into a skillet add a little salad oil and brown the pork. Add salt and pepper. Remove and drain excess grease. In the same pan, add a little more oil and the squash and brown the squash slightly. Add the pork and 2 cups of soup stock and continue cooking until squash is almost tender. Add 1 t. salt and monosodium glutamate. Cover and cook until the soup is absorbed. Serve immediately.

II. Squash with Shrimp Miso Sauce

> $1^2/_3$ lbs. squash
> $1/_2$ lb. small shrimp
> $1/_2$ lb. white *miso* paste
> *sake*
> $2^1/_2$ cups soup stock (No. 4)
> salt
> soy sauce
> sugar
> monosodium glutamate

Select a fresh tender skinned squash. Divide into 5 equal pieces. Into $2^1/_2$ cups of soup stock, add 1 t. salt, 2 t. soy sauce, 1 t. sugar and monosodium glutamate.

Bring to a boil, add the squash and over a low flame cook covered until the squash is tender. Allow to stand as is for about 20 minutes.

Mix the *miso* paste, 2 T. sugar, 2 T. *sake* and 1 T. water in a sauce pan. Shell, devein and mince the shrimp. Add to the *miso* and mix thoroughly. Cook this mixture until the shrimp is tender.

Place the squash on individual plates and pour the remaining sauce over the squash. Dress the squash with the shrimp *miso* sauce and serve while hot.

12. Shrimp, Taro and Spinach

> 5 taro*
> $2/_3$ lb. spinach
> 5 large shrimp
> $2^1/_2$ cups soup stock (No. 2 or 3)
> salt
> sugar
> soy sauce
> monosodium glutamate

Peel and remove both ends of the taro. (If using canned, this is not necessary.) In salted water, boil until it is almost tender. (A fork should not pierce it completely.) Drain. Rinse in cold water and drain again.

Cut the leaves from the spinach and drop into salted boiling water (1 t. salt to 5 cups water) until tender. Rinse in cold water and drain.

Shell the shrimp except for the tail and adjoining section and devein. Cut the shrimp down the back and open flat.

Bring the soup stock to a boil with $1^1/2$ t. salt and 1 T. sugar. When it boils, add the taro and continue boiling over a low flame with cover on. When the taro is almost tender, add the shrimp and 1 t. soy sauce. When the shrimp are tender, add the spinach. Over a strong flame, bring to a boil without cover.

Into a soup bowl, place the taro, shrimp and spinach and pour the soup over them. Serve immediately. It is pleasant to have it garnished in the spring with a pepper sprout and in the autumn with a slice of lemon.

13. How to Boil White Fish Fillet

Allow 1 piece of fish per person

1 lb. fish (sea bream, sole fish, sea perch)
sake
soy sauce
mirin

Mix 4 T. *sake*, 4 T. soy sauce and 3 T. *mirin* in a saucepan and bring to a boil. Add the fish and cover with a lid which fits inside the pan on the fish. Also cover with the saucepan lid. (This prevents evaporation.)

Boil until well flavored over a strong flame. During boiling, when the contents boil over, remove only the saucepan lid. Remove from fire. Serve on each plate with the sauce poured over the fish.

14. How to Cook Red Fish Fillet

Allow 1 piece of fish per person

$1^1/3$ lbs. fish (mackerel, sardine, bonito)
soy sauce
mirin
sake
sugar

Mix 6 T. soy sauce, 4 T. *mirin*, 4 T. *sake* and $1^1/2$ T. sugar. Cook as in the previous recipe except when the fish sauce boils up, turn the heat low and continue cooking for 5–6 minutes and remove the inner lid, continue cooking for 20 minutes. Serve the fish on individual plates.

STEAMED FOODS

I. Steamed Egg Custard

Custard ingredients
    8 eggs
    $1^1/_2$ cups soup stock (No. 2 or 3)
    $1^1/_2$ t. soy sauce
    $2/_3$ t. salt
    $2/_3$ t. sugar
    monosodium glutamate
Sauce ingredients
    3 ozs. bamboo shoots*
    3 ozs. carrots
    $1/_3$ oz. dried mushrooms
    a few string beans
    2 cups soup stock (No. 2 or 3)
    $1^1/_2$ t. soy sauce
    $2/_3$ t. salt
    $1^1/_2$ t. sugar
    monosodium glutamate
    cornstarch

To make the custard, mix the ingredients and see page 16 for steaming directions.

Cube ($1/_3$ in.) all the vegetables. Mix 2 cups soup stock, $1^1/_2$ t. soy sauce, $2/_3$ t. salt, $1^1/_2$ t. sugar and monosodium glutamate and bring to a boil. When the soup stock boils, add the vegetables and cook until tender. Add the dissolved cornstarch, cook until thickened, pour over the steamed egg and serve while hot.

2. Steamed Fish Fillet

    5 white fish fillets
    $2/_3$ lb. turnips

61

1¹/₂ T. egg white
1/2 lb. spinach
1 oz. ginger
salt
soy sauce
1 cup soup stock (No. 3)
cornstarch
monosodium glutamate

Salt the fish and allow to stand for 2 hours. Wash and wipe dry. Drop the spinach into boiling salted water and boil until tender. Rinse in cold water and drain. Arrange in order and cut into 1¹/₂ in. lengths to form "clumps" of spinach.

Peel and grate the turnips, add the egg white, 2/3 t. salt and monosodium glutamate and mix well.

Into shallow individual dishes, place 1 piece of fish, on the top place 1 "clump" of spinach and 1/5 of the turnip sauce. Steam for 20 minutes and serve while hot with the following sauce;

Mix 1 cup soup stock, 2/3 t. salt, 2/3 t. soy sauce, monosodium glutamate and cornstarch. Cook until thickened and pour over the steamed fish. If desired, add grated ginger juice.

3. Stuffed Pumpkin

1 pumpkin (about 1¹/₃ lbs.)
1 square of soy bean curd
2 ozs. ground chicken meat
1/3 oz. carrots
1/3 oz. dried mushrooms
1 cup chicken soup stock
salt
sugar
monosodium glutamate
cornstarch

Cut the 1/4 top of the pumpkin off to form a cover. Remove the seeds and sprinkle well with salt. In a cheesecloth remove the liquid from the soy bean curd. Soften the dried mushrooms in water until soft. Cut the dried mushrooms and carrots into narrow strips. Mash the soy bean

62

Stuffed Pumpkin

Unadama—mushi, Steamed Egg and Eel

1) pumpkin
2) soy bean curd
   chicken meat

   dried mushroom
   carrot

3) egg

4) broiled eel

curd until no lumps are left and add 2/3 t. salt, 2 t. sugar, monosodium glutamate, carrots, dried mushrooms and chicken. Mix well and fill the pumpkin. Steam until tender. (Don't forget the cover when steaming. It is not to be put in place until the pumpkin is served.)

Mix 1 cup soup stock, 1/2 t. salt, monosodium glutamate and cornstarch and cook until thickened. Put the pumpkin cover in place and pour this gravy over all.

4. Unadama-mushi, Steamed Egg and Eel

To make egg mixture
> 7 eggs
> 1 1/4 cups soup stock (No. 2 or 3)
> 1 1/2 t. soy sauce
> 2/3 t. salt
> 1/2 t. sugar
> monosodium glutamate
> 1 can of broiled eels (*unagi no kabayaki*)

To make sauce
> 1 1/2 cups soup stock (No. 1 or 2)
> soy sauce
> monosodium glutamate
> salt
> cornstarch

Mix the ingredients for the egg mixture together. Cut the eel 1/3 in. in length. Add the cut up eel and mix well. Steam for 40–50 minutes in a 1 in. thick square mold. (A cake pan could be used.) When it is done, remove from mold and cut into 10 or 15 equal pieces.

Mix 1 1/2 cups soup stock with 1/2 t. salt, 1 t. sugar, monosodium glutamate and cornstarch. Cook until thickened.

In individual dishes, pour the sauce on the top of the egg and eel. Serve immediately.

63

SUNOMONO AND AEMONO, SALADS

I. Cucumbers and Shrimp

> 1 lb. cucumbers
> 1/2 lb. shrimp (1/2 of this if using canned)
> salt
> vinegar
> sugar
> monosodium glutamate
> 1 oz. ginger

Cut the cucumbers into 2 in. in length chunks and then slice the chunks very thin lengthwise. Salt and mix. Allow to stand for about 20 minutes until they become soft. Mix again, drain and mix with 1 T. vinegar. Mix well. Drain the liquid by squeezing the cucumbers gently.

Devein the shrimp and insert skewers through the back to keep them straight during boiling as shown on page 30. Boil in salted water until tender. Remove the skewers and shell. Slice lengthwise. (If canned shrimp are used, no cooking is necessary.)

Mix 3 T. vinegar, 1 t. salt, 1 T. sugar and monosodium glutamate and then add the cucumbers and shrimp. Mince the ginger very fine, leave in the water until bleached and drain. Arrange the cucumbers and shrimp in individual small bowls and garnish with ginger.

2. "Maple" Salad

> 2/3 lb. radish
> 1 small carrot
> 1/3 lb. cucumbers
> a few dried mushrooms
> 1/2 lb. shrimp
> 3 eggs
> salt

64

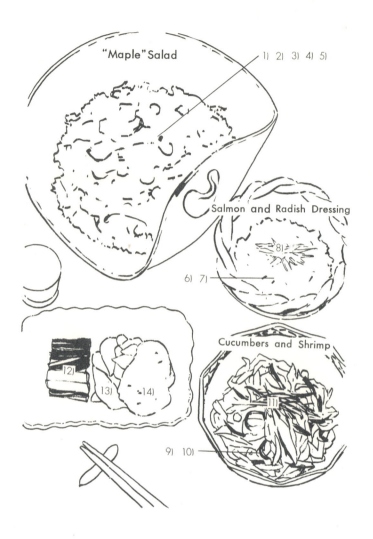

"Maple" Salad   1) 2) 3) 4) 5)

Salmon and Radish Dressing

6) 7)   8)

Cucumbers and Shrimp

9) 10)   11)

12) 13) 14)

1)	carrot	4)	dried mushroom
2)	egg	5)	cucumber
3)	radish		
6)	salmon	8)	ginger
7)	radish		
9)	shrimp	11)	ginger
10)	cucumber		
12)	green onion	14)	*miso* and vinegar
13)	raw red foot of clams		

vinegar
sugar
monosodium glutamate

Peel and cut the radish and carrot into $1^1/2$ in. strips. Cut the cucumbers in the same manner without peeling. Salt and allow to stand until the cucumbers, carrot and radish become soft. Press out the liquid. Soften the dried mushrooms in cold water and slice into thin strips. Mix cucumbers, carrot, radish and dried mushrooms with $1^1/2$ T. vinegar.

Devein the shrimp and insert skewers through the back to keep them straight during boiling as shown on page 30. Boil in salted water until tender. Remove the skewers and shell. Slice lengthwise.

Beat the eggs. Add 1 t. salt and 1 T. sugar. Stir while frying to make a granulated finished mixture. Force the egg mixture through a sieve while hot and allow to cool. Add 2 T. vinegar and mix.

To the drained vegetables add $1^1/2$ T. vinegar, mix well and squeeze.

Add vegetables and shrimp, to the egg mixture gently. Arrange the salad on individual plates in the form of a maple leaf. These colors are to suggest the fall coloring of the maple leaf.

3. Salmon and Radish

1 lb. radish
1 small can of salmon
5 Japanese pepper sprouts or minced ginger
vinegar
salt
sugar
monosodium glutamate

Remove the bones from the salmon and drain. Peel and grate the radish. Drain the juice from the grated radish. Season the grated radish with 2 T. vinegar, $1^1/2$ t. salt, 1 T. sugar and monosodium glutamate. Mix this with flaked salmon.

Serve on individual plates, garnished with Japanese pepper sprout or minced ginger.

4. Eggplant Dressed with Mustard

$1^1/2$ lbs. eggplant

65

1^1/$_2$ t. mustard
salt
vinegar
monosodium glutamate

Cut the eggplant into eighths without peeling and then make cuts through the skin side very fine. Salt as you slice to prevent discoloration. When the eggplant have become soft, press to drain. Add 1 T. vinegar, mix again and drain off excess liquid.

To 1^1/$_2$ t. mustard, add 1 T. vinegar, 1^1/$_2$ T. soy sauce and monosodium glutamate. This is "salad dressing" for the eggplant. Mix well Serve on individual plates and eat immediately.

5. Spiced Eggplant

1^1/$_2$ lbs. eggplant
2 T. white sesame seeds
1 bunch of green onions
1 red pepper
soy sauce
sugar
monosodium glutamate

Remove the stem from the eggplant and cut into 8 lengthwise. Allow to stand in water for 30 minutes and drain. Arrange on a plate and sprinkle 2 T. soy sauce on them. Steam until tender. Drain and cool.

Over a hot fire, put the sesame seeds into an ungreased pan and heat until they start "jumping". Remove from heat and grind in a mortar. (Blender will do fine.) Add the minced green onions and minced red pepper, 2 T. soy sauce, ^{2}/$_3$ t. sugar and monosodium glutamate to the sesame seeds.

Arrange the eggplant on a large plate, sprinkle ^{1}/$_2$ of the sesame seeds mixture on the eggplant. On the top of this, arrange the remaining half of the eggplant and sesame seeds in like manner. Serve immediately.

6. Green Onions and Round Clams

^{3}/$_4$ lb. raw red foot of clams

66

3/4 lb. small green onions or asparagus (canned)
5 ozs. white *miso* paste
sugar
sake
monosodium glutamate

Wash the clams, drain and cut into bite size. (If canned clam is used, merely cut.)

Dip green onions quickly in and out of boiling salted water. Allow to stand in the cold water until cool. Cut the end of the green part and with knife against a board, push the water out of the leaves. Cut into about 2 in. in length. Blend together the *miso* paste, 2 T. sugar and 3 T. *sake*. Over a low flame, bring to a boil stirring continuously. Pour into a bowl and chill. Add 1¹/₂ T. vinegar and monosodium glutamate.

Serve in individual bowls with the dressing poured over the clams.

7. Radish and Ham Golden Miso Salad

1 lb. radish
1/4 lb. sliced ham
1 egg
5 ozs. white *miso* paste
salt
sugar
sake
vinegar
monosodium glutamate

Peel and cut the radish 1¹/₂ in. in length, then slice into strips. Salt and allow to stand for 20 minutes until soft. Squeeze. Mix with 1¹/₂ T. vinegar. Squeeze once more. Slice the ham also into strips about the same size as the radish.

Mix *miso* paste with 2¹/₂ T. sugar and 3 T. *sake* and heat till thickened. Chill. The egg yolk should be seasoned with monosodium glutamate and be added to the *miso* mixture.

Dress the radish and ham with the *miso* dressing prepared as above on individual dishes.

67

8. Spinach with White Sesame Seeds

2 lbs. spinach
3 T. white sesame seeds
soy sauce
sugar
monosodium glutamate

Into salted boiling water, dip $1/5$th of the spinach by the roots and hold until soft. Rinse in cold water and drain. Repeat with the rest of the spinach.

Arrange so that it can be cut into $3/4$ in. in length pieces. **Mix** with $1^1/_2$ T. soy sauce. Crush the sesame seeds in a mortar, after heating in an ungreased pan until they start "jumping". Mix with $2^1/_2$ T. soy sauce, $1^1/_2$ t. sugar and monosodium glutamate. Dress the spinach with white sesame seed mixture well.

To serve, arrange on individual plates.

9. Cuttlefish and Bamboo Shoot Salad

1 lb. cuttlefish
$1/2$ lb. bamboo shoots*
1 T. sea urchin (bottled)
1 egg yolk
1 *yuzu* or lemon
salt
vinegar
monosodium glutamate

Cut the bamboo shoots into $1^1/_4$ in. long.

Cut the cuttlefish legs off. Peel the skin off. Dip quickly in and out of boiling water. Put into cold water to cool. Drain. Cut the same as bamboo shoots. Mix cuttlefish, bamboo shoots and $1^1/_2$ T. vinegar well and drain.

Mix the sea urchin paste with $1/2$ T. vinegar and the egg yolk. Strain through a sieve. Dress the bamboo shoots and cuttlefish with the sea urchin mixture. Add salt and monosodium glutamate to taste. To serve, arrange with *yuzu,* or lemon on individual dishes.

10. Pork and String Bean Salad

2/3 lb. string beans
1/2 lb. pork
2 squares of soy bean curd
2 T. white sesame seeds
salt
sugar
soy sauce
monosodium glutamate
2 T. soup stock (No. 3)

Wrap the soy bean curd in cheesecloth and place between 2 wooden boards. Put a weight on the top to press out the water. Parch the sesame seeds and crush in a mortar (blender). Add 2 T. soup stock, 1½ t. salt, 2 T. sugar, 1 t. soy sauce and monosodium glutamate. Mix well. (This mixture can be put through a food mill, or sieve if wanted.)

Cut the pork into 2 in. narrow strips and salt. Drop into boiling water and boil until tender, chill and drain.

String and drop the beans into boiling salted water. When tender, rinse in cold water and drain. Cut into 2 in. strips the same as pork. Sprinkle with 1 T. soy sauce and squeeze.

Add the pork and the string beans to the mixture and mix well, to serve arrange on individual plates.

11. Cucumber and Crab Meat Salad

1 lb. cucumbers
1/2 can of crab meat
1 oz. ginger
vinegar
soy sauce
sugar
salt
monosodium glutamate

Slice the unpeeled cucumbers as thin as possible. Salt and allow to stand for 20 minutes. Squeeze to remove the liquid, add 1 T. vinegar and gently squeeze again. Break the crab meat apart into small pieces.

69

Mix 3 T. vinegar, $1/2$ t. salt, $1^1/2$ t. soy sauce, 1 T. sugar and mono-sodium glutamate. Add the cucumbers and crab meat and mix well. Divide into equal portions and place in individual dishes. Garnish with a few finely cut strips of ginger and serve.

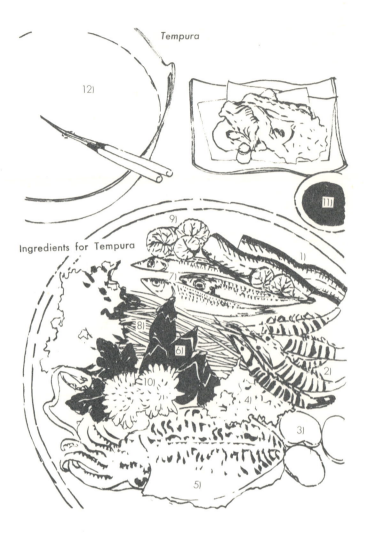

Tempura

Ingredients for Tempura

1) sea-eel

2) shrimp

3) scallop ligament

4) *shungiku*

5) cuttlefish

6) eggplant

7) sillago

8) trefoil

9) strawberry-geranium

10) chrysanthemum flower

11) *tempura* sauce

12) frying oil

FRIED FOODS (DEEP-FAT)

I. Tempura

Tempura is a dish of fish and vegetables, changing with the season.

To prepare the batter, mix 1 1/4 cups soft (cake flour consistency) wheat flour, 4 T. rice flour and 4 T. cornstarch with 1 1/3 cups water and 1 egg as follows. Beat the egg yolk and add 1/2 of the water. Add the wheat flour, rice flour and cornstarch and mix from the outside to the center of the bowl quickly. Add the remaining water and stir. If there are lumps, it makes no difference. Last, add stiffly beaten egg white. Make the batter just before using.

It is best to use sesame seed oil, or 2/3 sesame seed oil and 1/3 salad oil at a temperature of 360°F. (Salad oil by itself is too mild.)

To make *tempura* sauce, use 3 parts soup stock (made of *katsuobushi* dried bonito fillet and *konbu* seaweed), 1 part *mirin* and 1 part soy sauce and bring to a boil. When served at the table, monosodium glutamate and salt may be added.

Usually *tempura* is eaten as it is fried, but if not possible, each person's quantity can be dished up on individual dishes. In another small bowl, serve individual servings of the *tempura* sauce. On the third dish, place the grated radish and ginger to be put, by the individual eating, into the soup as he dips the *tempura* before eating.

10 fresh shrimp
3 large mussels
5 sea-eels
5 sillagoes
1/2 lb. cuttlefish or squid
30 trefoils or greens
5 chrysanthemum leaves
5 chrysanthemum flowers
7 ozs. *Shungiku* (edible chrysanthemum leaves) or green vegetables
1/2 cup fresh scallop ligaments
1 eggplant

Whatever vegetables or fish are available is usually made more tempting by "temperizing".

Shell except for the tail and adjoining segment, devein and prepare the shrimp as shown in the following figure. If one wishes to use sea-eels, prepare as directed on page 50. If the cuttlefish legs are attached, remove. Slit and peel off the 2 outer layers of skin. (The fish man will do this for you if you ask.) Wash and wipe dry. Cut into $1^1/_2 \times 1^1/_4$ in. oblongs. Clean the mussels and slice crossgrain into 4 slices. Wipe dry. Wash and remove entrails and bones of the sillagoes leaving 2 slices of flesh, one from either side. Wipe dry. Prepare the trefoils as shown on page 15. Wash and drain thoroughly the chrysanthemums. Use the tender leaves of the edible chrysanthemums, wash and drain thoroughly. Clean and slice the eggplant into $1/_4$ in. slices. Arrange the vegetables and fish in an attractive manner on a large plate. Save the legs of the cuttlefish, the trimmed ends of the

1)

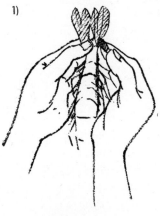

Tempura shrimp

1)   To remove the tendon which is between the "tail", spread the tail apart and pull the tendon out with the fingers.
2)   To remove the water from the "tail" shells, press each shell between the thumb and forefinger and push the water out.
3)   To straighten the shrimp, bend it backwards until it will lay straight when released.

2)

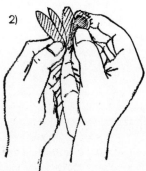

3)

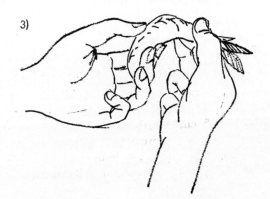

72

trefoils, etc. They are chopped, mixed and fried last by the spoonful.

To fry, into a large skillet or deep-fat fryer, add enough oil to completely cover the ingredients that are put in. When the oil reaches 350°—360°F (or when a small drop of batter cooks thoroughly in 60 seconds), take the ingredients, using first the ones without strong flavours and one at a time, dip into the batter and then into the oil to fry. When nicely browned, remove and drain the excess oil on brown paper, or on a rack with a receptacle underneath to catch the oil. Be careful when dropping the spoonful of chopped leftovers to fry. If you slide it in from the side, the oil will not splatter. Serve immediately. If all is not eaten at this time, save and use later. See page 82.

2. Ganmodoki, Fried Soy Bean Curd and Vegetables

3 squares of soy bean curd
2 ozs. carrots
1/6 oz. dried mushrooms
1 egg
mustard
salt
sugar
frying oil
monosodium glutamate

Remove the water from the soy bean curd by placing in a cheesecloth and squeeze. Cut the carrots into narrow strips. Soften the dried mushrooms in cold water and cut the same as the carrots.

Place the soy bean curd into a bowl and with the hands form it into a firm ball. Add 1 t. salt, 2/3 T. sugar, 1 egg, monosodium glutamate, carrots and dried mushrooms. Mix well and form 15 round patties. Fry without batter, as shown above (page 73). When fried, serve on a paper towel or paper napkin which has been placed on a dish. Add a small amount of mustard. In a side dish, place soy sauce for dipping.

3. Tobadofu, Fried Soy Bean Curd

3 squares of soy bean curd
frying oil

1 egg white

1 1/2 ozs. ginger, grated

1 cup soup stock (No. 2 or 3)

bread or cracker crumbs

soy sauce

salt

sugar

vinegar

cornstarch

monosodium glutamate

Place the soy bean curd for 1 hour between 2 boards with a weight on the top to press the liquid out. Cut into $2 \times 1/2$ in. oblongs. Into the egg white, add 1/2 T. water. Dip the soy bean curd into the egg mixture and then into bread crumbs and fry.

To prepare vinegar flavoured gravy, mix 1 cup soup stock, 2/3 T. soy sauce, 1/2 t. salt, 2 T. vinegar, 1/2 T. sugar and monosodium glutamate. Add dissolved cornstarch and thicken over fire.

To serve, place the soy bean curd on individual dishes, cover with gravy and garnish with grated ginger.

4. Fish with Seven Spices

1 1/2 lbs. mackerel

2 T. white sesame seeds

1/3 oz. green onions or onions (soaked in cold water)

1/2 lb. radish

2 *zingiber mioga* (Latin) flowers

2 red peppers

crushed Japanese pepper

1/2 lemon

salt

soy sauce

frying oil

monosodium glutamate

Wash, remove the entrails, head and tail of the mackerel and slice crosswise into 1 in. thick pieces. Drain. Fry and place on a piece of absorbent paper on individual dishes.

To prepare the spices, grate the radish, slice the green onions and *zingiber mioga* flowers into thin rounds, mince the red peppers, heat and grind the sesame seeds. Place a heap of each of them on a large plate. Place the lemon juice in a small dish. At the table, add soy sauce and any spice one wishes to the lemon juice. Eat the fish as it is dipped into the lemon juice, soy sauce and spice mixture.

5. Fried Pork Balls

2/3 lb. ground pork
1/3 oz. dried mushrooms
1 bunch of green onions or onions
1 egg
soy sauce
salt
vinegar
sugar
sake
frying oil
2 red peppers
1/3 oz. *katsuobushi* dried bonito fillet
1/3 oz. *konbu* seaweed (used for seasoning soup stock only)

Mix well the pork, dried mushrooms (softened in cold water and minced), minced green onions, 2/3 T. soy sauce, 1/2 t. salt, 1 t. sugar and egg. Form 1/2 in. size balls and fry in deep-fat.

Prepare the sauce by mixing 4 T. *sake*, 4 T. soy sauce, 3 T. vinegar, 1 T. sugar, 2 red peppers, 1/3 oz. dried bonito fillet and 1/3 oz. *konbu* seaweed. Bring to a boil and strain off the residue.

Into the sauce place the meat balls and allow to stand. Remove the meat balls after 6 hours or more and serve on individual plates.

6. Fried Salmon Balls

5 ozs. canned salmon
2/3 lb. potatoes
1 small carrot
1/2 oz. ginger
2 eggs

cornstarch
1/3 oz. dried mushrooms
frying oil
lettuce
salt
soy sauce
vinegar
sugar
monosodium glutamate

Mince the salmon and mash the cooled potatoes. Boil the carrot and after softening the dried mushrooms in cold water, cut them into strips. Add to them minced ginger, 1 t. salt, 2 eggs and monosodium glutamate. Form balls about 1 in. in size. Coat with cornstarch and fry.

Usually "*sanbaizu*" made of 1 part vinegar, 1 part soy sauce and 1 part *mirin* is used for dipping the meat balls in, but I prefer 3 T. soy sauce, $2^1/2$ T. vinegar and 2 t. sugar with monosodium glutamate. Serve the fish balls with a side dish of the above sauce.

7. Senbei (Cracker) Tempura

Suitable fish is sillago, sea bream, flounder, sole fish, etc.

5 fish fillets or small fish
5 *senbei* salted Japanese crackers
1 egg
frying oil
soup stock (No. 3)
mirin
soy sauce
5 ozs. radish
1 oz. ginger

Wash and drain the fish. Crush the crackers with a rolling pin, or in a blender. This must be very, very fine, like powder. To make the batter, beat the egg with 1/2 T. water. Dip the fish into the egg and then into the crackers and fry. Drain the excess oil on paper.

Make *tempura* sauce. See page 71. Serve with the sauce, grated radish and grated ginger.

Fried Shrimp (in the shape of chrysanthemum)

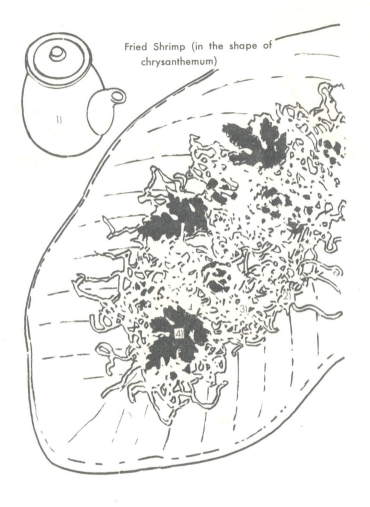

1) *tempura sauce*   3) shrimp
2) *harusame*   4) chrysanthemum leaf

8. Fried Vegetables

1/4 lb. burdock root*
2 1/2 ozs. carrots
1/3 lb. sweet potatoes*
1 oz. string beans
2/3 cup water
1 1/4 cups soft wheat flour
frying oil
soy sauce
salt

To prepare the batter, mix 1 1/4 cups soft wheat flour with 2/3 cup water and 1/2 t. salt. See page 71.

Peel the burdock root and cut into 2 in. lengths and boil until tender. Prepare the carrots, sweet potatoes and string beans and cut into the same size as the burdock root, but do not boil. Mix the vegetables well and divide into 20 equal parts. One by one put the vegetable "balls" into the batter. Mix, remove and fry in deep-fat. Make a sauce of 3 T. soy sauce, 2 1/2 T. vinegar and 2 t. sugar and monosodium glutamate to serve in individual side dishes for dipping the fried vegetables.

9. Fried Shrimp (in the shape of chrysanthemum)

1 1/2 ozs. shrimp
1 egg white
cornstarch
salt
monosodium glutamate
frying oil
a carton of *harusame* noodles
radish
ginger
soup stock (No. 3)
mirin
soy sauce

Shell and devein the shrimp. Wash and wipe dry. Grind in motor and mix with egg white, 2/3 t. salt, 1 1/2 t. cornstarch and monosodium glutamate. Make balls 4/5 in. in diameter. Cut the *harusame* noodles into

77

2 in. lengths and dip one side of the shrimp balls into the noodles allowing many of the 2 in. noodles to stick forming a flower form. **Fry** in deep-fat. To serve, place on absorbent paper on a dish, with **a** side dish of *tempura* sauce. See page 71.

10. Skewer Nibblers

10 shrimp
5 sillagoes
3 ozs. scallops
3 sea-eels
10 small oysters
1/3 lb. pork
1/3 lb. beef
1/3 lb. chicken meat
2/3 lb. cuttlefish or squid
4 T. soft wheat flour
1 egg
4 T. bread crumbs
1 T. green *nori* seaweed
2 sheets of *nori* seaweed
3 large dried mushrooms
5 small onions
5 Brussel sprouts
5 quail's eggs
2 green peppers
4 ozs. cheese
1 oz. green onions
2/3 oz. ginger
1 oz. seasoned sea urchin
soy sauce
salt
mustard
frying oil
sake

Use any other available fish and vegetable according to the season. Shell, devein and wash the shrimp. Insert skewers. Salt. Dip into wheat flour, beaten egg and then into bread crumbs. Fry.

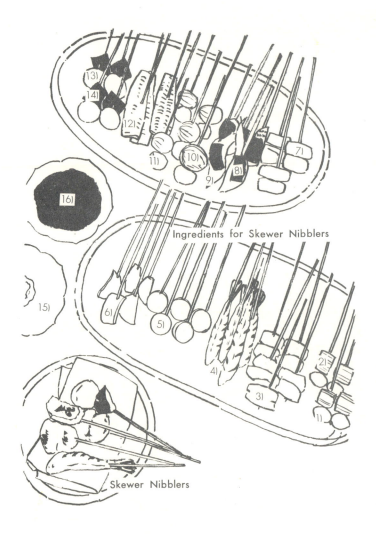

Ingredients for Skewer Nibblers

Skewer Nibblers

1)	gingko nuts	9)	sillago
2)	green onion	10)	onion
3)	scallop ligament and green	11)	pork
	nori seaweed	12)	sea-eel
4)	shrimp	13)	quail's egg
5)	cheese	14)	dried mushroom
6)	cuttlefish	15)	mustard
7)	chicken meat	16)	Worcestershire sauce
8)	*nori* seaweed		

Split the sillagoes and remove the bones, entrails and tail. Cut into 2 in. bites, cover with *nori* seaweed, insert a skewer and dip into batter as on page 71. Slice each scallop crosswise into 4, dress with sea urchin paste, sprinkle green *nori* seaweed, insert a skewer, dip in batter and fry.

Prepare the sea-eel as on page 50, dip in batter and fry.

Wipe the oysters dry and salt, insert a skewer, coat with wheat flour, beaten egg and then with bread crumbs and fry. Use only the body of the cuttlefish, washed and cut into squares ($1^{1}/_{2}$ in.). Insert a skewer. Dip in batter and fry.

Allow the chicken and the beef bite size chunks to soak in an equal proportion of *sake* and soy sauce. Insert a skewer into a piece of beef and 1 onion (parboiled in salted water). Insert a skewer into 1 piece of chicken and 1 Brussel sprout. Dip beef and chicken skewers into beaten egg, cover with bread crumbs and fry.

Cut the pork into $1^{1}/_{2} \times 2^{1}/_{3}$ in. rectangular and salt. Cut the green onions and ginger into strips. Roll a few of green onions and ginger with pork. Insert a skewer and fry.

Hard boil the quail's eggs, shell and salt. Soften the dried mushrooms in water and cut each into 3 pieces. Insert a skewer into 1 quail's egg and 1 dried mushroom, coat with cornstarch and fry. Cube the cheese and insert a skewer. Dip into beaten egg and bread crumbs.

Serve with salt, vinegar, soy sauce, Worcestershire sauce, mustard and catsup for dipping.

RICE

Cooking Method

Rice differs in its moisture content depending upon 1) the length of time since harvesting and 2) the locality where it was grown.

Following is a standard table in Japan that can be used which allows for the variants.

Season	Water	Rice
November—middle of December	8 cups	8 cups
End of December—March	8 4/5 cups	8 cups
April—June (rainy season)	9 1/5 cups	8 cups
July—September	9 3/5 cups	8 cups
End of September—end of October	10 cups	8 cups

1. How to Cook the Rice

In all of the following 8 cups of rice are used. This is enough to feed 10 Japanese people. Non-Japanese may not eat this much.

One hour before cooking the rice, wash it well and drain.

Put the rice and water in a deep pan (a pressure cooker without using the pressure can be used) and mix well. Bring to a boil over a strong flame while covered. When it boils, turn the flame as low as possible and simmer for 3 minutes. Bring again to a boil over a little stronger flame and as the water diminishes, turn the flame lower. When the water is nearly gone (about 20 minutes), turn the flame strong for 1–2 seconds and remove from fire still covered. Allow to stand for 7 minutes. Serve.

When you remove the lid to serve, if the rice has "risen", you can be sure you have made delicious rice.

2. Sekihan, Red Rice

8 cups *mochi* rice (glutinous rice)

1 cup *azuki* red beans
4 T. black sesame seeds
2 T. salt

Wash the rice and allow to stand overnight in water. (If in a hurry, warm the rice in the water in the sun.) If for a ceremonial occasion, a little red food coloring can be added. Wash the red beans and allow to stand in water. Cook until tender with the cover on. Drain the rice and red beans. The rice and red beans are mixed together and steamed for about 40 minutes. During the steaming, sprinkle a little of the salted water in which the red beans were cooked, 2–3 times on the top of the rice. Have the flame as strong as possible to give the rice as much moisture as possible. (If using red coloring, use salted water to sprinkle on the rice.) When steamed put into a covered container to keep warm.

Put the sesame seeds and salt into a hot ungreased skillet until they start to "jump" and sprinkle on the top of the individual plates with the rice and red beans.

3. Sushi Rice

a. Kanto Type Sushi (Tokyo Sushi)

To cook the rice
8 cups rice
1 cup *mirin*
1 2/3 ozs. *konbu* seaweed (used for seasoning soup stock)
To season the rice
1 1/4 cups *yamabukizu* sweet vinegar
3 T. salt
1 t. monosodium glutamate
(If this is not available, substitute 4/5 cup regular vinegar with 3 T. sugar, 3 t. salt and 1 t. monosodium glutamate.)

Wash and drain the rice 1 hour before cooking.

Bring to a boil the water, *konbu* seaweed and *mirin*. Remove the *konbu* seaweed and add the rice. Mix well and bring to a boil over medium flame. When it boils, reduce the flame to a very low flame. Allow to stand for 3 minutes. Turn the flame up some and as the water diminishes, lower the flame. When the water has disappeared, turn off the fire and allow to stand 4–6 minutes. Remove the rice to a broad, shallow pan. While adding the sweet vinegar mixture to the rice, quickly mix and fan to cool.

Kanto rice is used for making *nigiri sushi.*

Kansai and *Kyushu* types of *sushi* rice are used for *sushi* sandwiches, *chirashi sushi* and *nori maki sushi.*

Proportion of rice for both *Osaka* (*Kansai*) and West Japan (*Kyushu*)

8 cups water
8 cups rice
$4/5$ cup *mirin*
$12/3$ ozs. *konbu* seaweed

After cooking the rice add the following seasonings for the type of *sushi* desired.

b. **Kansai Type (Osaka Seasonings)**

$4/5$ cup vinegar
6 T. sugar
3 t. salt
1 t. monosodium glutamate

c. **West Japan Seasonings**

$4/5$ cup vinegar
8 T. sugar
3 t. salt
1 t. monosodium glutamate

Dressed Rice

This is served in bowls with a lid.

I. Tendon, Tempura on Rice

4 cups rice
5 shrimp
3 sillagoes
5 mixed leftover patties of cuttlefish and trefoil
1 cuttlefish

Ingredients for sauce

4 T. *mirin*

4 T. *sake*
4 T. soy sauce
2 T. sugar

To cook the rice, see page 80.
To make *tempura* (shrimp, cuttlefish, sillago and mixed cuttlefish and trefoil), see page 71.

Bring to a boil the *mirin* and *sake* until it becomes thick. Add the soy sauce and sugar, bring once more to a boil and remove from fire.

Into a deep bowl with a cover, place individual servings of rice. Dip the fried foods quickly in and out of the hot sauce and place on the top of the rice. Pour 1 T. sauce over the fried foods. Cover and serve.

2. Three Colored Rice (makes 3 servings)

a) 2 2/5 cups rice
    2 3/4 cups water
    1 T. soy sauce
    1/2 t. salt

Mix the above ingredients in a saucepan with cover and see directions for cooking rice (page 80).

b) 1/2 lb. ground chicken meat or sliced
    2 T. *sake*
    1 T. soy sauce
    1 T. water
    1 t. sugar

Mix the above ingredients and while stirring, cook until the chicken meat is tender.

c) 3 eggs
    1/2 t. salt
    2/3 t. sugar
    monosodium glutamate

Mix the above ingredients and cook while stirring so that the egg when done has a granulated appearance.

d) 1 bunch of watercress or turnip green tips
    1/4 t. salt
    monosodium glutamate

Dip watercress quickly in and out of boiling water, rinse in cold water and squeeze with hands. Mince and squeeze once more. Mix with the salt and monosodium glutamate.

e) red pickled ginger
    Cut the ginger into fine strips.

Into a deep rice bowl, place individual servings making the top flat. On the top of the rice, arrange the chicken, eggs and watercress in a manner similar to the picture opposite page 90. ˙ Place a small amount of red ginger in the center.

3. Soboro Donburi

    4 cups rice
    1 1/2 squares of soy bean curd
    3 ozs. ground beef
    1 green onion
    3 ozs. carrots
    5 stalks of parsley
    2 eggs
    salad oil
    soy sauce
    salt
    monosodium glutamate
    sugar

To cook the rice, see page 80.

Drain the liquid off the soy bean curd by wrapping in cheesecloth and squeezing. Mince the green onion, parsley and carrots. In a heated skillet with 2 T. salad oil, place the vegetables and brown. When the vegetables are brown, add the beef. When the beef is browned, add the soy bean curd and stir while cooking. Add 3 T. soy sauce, 2/3 t. salt, 1 T. sugar and monosodium glutamate and mix well. Remove from fire and while it is cooling, continue to mix for 20–30 seconds. Beat the eggs and add to the mixture. Place once more on the fire and stirr

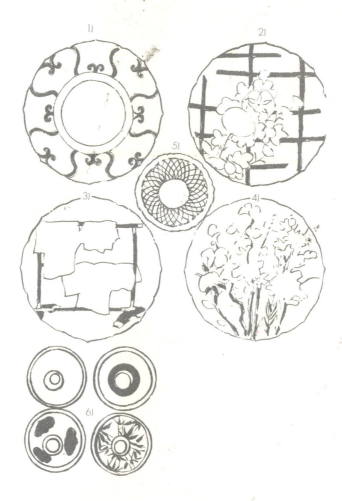

1) ornamental dish   4) ornamental dish

2) ornamental dish   5) fruit or dessert dish

3) ornamental dish   6) rice bowl

constantly, until the eggs are cooked.

Into a deep rice bowl, place individual servings of rice. On the rice place the soy bean curd-beef-egg mixture.

4. Oyako Donburi, Chicken and Egg on Rice

    4 cups rice
    2/3 lb. thinly sliced chicken meat
    5 eggs
    5 large dried mushrooms
    1/2 lb. onions
    2 sheets of *nori* seaweed
    1/3 cup *mirin*
    1/3 cup *sake*
    1/3 cup soy sauce
    3 1/2 T. sugar
    1/2 cup soup stock (No. 3)
    monosodium glutamate

To cook the rice, see page 80.

Bring the *mirin* and *sake* to a boil and cook until thickened slightly. Add the soy sauce, sugar and soup stock to the above mixture and bring to a boil once more. Soak the dried mushrooms in cold water to soften. Cut into strips. Half the onions and slice thinly. Slice the chicken into small thin pieces, the size of an almond. Divide these ingredients into 5 equal portions. Hold the seaweed over the flame for a minute to crisp it and break in small pieces with the hands.

Fill individual large rice bowls with rice and replace the cover. Into a small skillet, put 1/5 of the soup and 1/5 of the onions, chicken and dried mushrooms. When all are tender, reduce the flame and add 1 beaten egg. When the egg is cooked, remove from fire and place on the top of the rice. Sprinkle with bits of seaweed. Cover. Repeat for 5 dishes of rice. Serve.

5. Na Meshi, Green Rice

    4 cups rice
    1 bunch of greens; parsley or edible chrysanthemum leaves
    salt
    monosodium glutamate

To cook the rice, see page 80.

The greens used in this dish must be cooked in boiling water until tender, being careful to retain green color. Rinse in cold water and squeeze out the water. Cut in short pieces, sprinkle with 2/3 t. salt and monosodium glutamate. The prepared greens are mixed in the rice.

Serve in large rice bowls with covers.

6. Takenoko Meshi, Rice and Bamboo Shoots

    4 cups rice
    1 1/3 lbs. bamboo shoots*
Ingredients for boiling bamboo shoots
    4/5 cup soup stock (No. 3)
    1 1/2 T. soy sauce
    1 1/2 T. *sake*
    1 1/2 t. sugar
    1/3 t. salt
    monosodium glutamate

Wash and drain the rice 1 hour before cooking.

Cut the bamboo shoots in half, then slice into narrow strips. Add to the soup stock ingredients and cook until well flavored. Drain the soup but do not discard. Keep the bamboo shoots warm. Into the soup (that the bamboo shoots were cooked in), add 2/3 T. soy sauce, 2 T. *sake* and enough water to bring the entire volume to 4 1/2 cups. Add 1/3 t. salt, 1/2 t. sugar and 4 cups of rice. Mix well. See page 80 for cooking method of rice. When the rice is cooked, add the bamboo shoots, mix well and serve in individual large rice bowls with covers.

7. Nikomi Meshi, Rice and Vegetables

    4 cups rice
    4 1/2 cups water
    2 ozs. burdock roots*
    3 ozs. carrots
    1 oz. dried white bait fish (lancelet)
    1 bunch of *shirataki* (long *konnyaku*)
    soy sauce
    salt
    monosodium glutamate

86

Wash and drain the rice 1 hour before cooking.

Cut the carrots and burdock into 1 in. long narrow strips (julienne). Place the burdock in water for about 30 minutes to remove the acridness. After 30 minutes, bring the burdock to a boil, rinse in cold water and drain. Cut the *shirataki* into 4/5 in. lengths. Wash, bring to a boil and drain. Wash the dried fish and drain. Mix the rice, carrots, burdock, *shirataki*, dried fish, 4¹/₂ cups of water, 1¹/₂ T. soy sauce, ²/₃ T. salt and monosodium glutamate. See page 80 for cooking method of rice. When done, mix lightly the vegetables and rice in the pan, place into individual bowls with covers and serve.

8. Milk Rice Gruel (makes 2 servings)

> 12 ozs. cooked rice
> 2 cups milk
> 1 oz. green onions
> salt
> monosodium glutamate

Mix the rice and milk well until there are no large lumps left. Cook covered for 1 hour over a low flame. After 30 minutes of cooking, add the salt and monosodium glutamate. Just before taking from fire, add the minced green onions. Serve while hot.

9. Tamago Zosui, Egg and Milk Rice Gruel

> 12 ozs. cooked rice
> 1/₄ cup chopped scallions
> 2 eggs
> 2 cups soup stock (No. 3)
> soy sauce
> monosodium glutamate

Place the scallions on the bottom of the saucepan, place the rice on the top of that and the soup stock on the top of the rice. (Vary the amount of soup stock as desired for softer consistency.) After 1 hour cooking over a low flame, add 1¹/₂ T. soy sauce, quickly mix and continue cooking for 30 minutes. Remove from fire, add 2 well beaten eggs and mix thoroughly. When the egg is partly coagulated, serve in individual large rice bowls. Makes 2 servings.

10. Tori Gayu, Chicken Rice Gruel

5 ozs. cubed ($1/3$ in.) chicken meat
1 cup rice
salt
soy sauce
8 cups chicken soup stock
1 green onion, minced
monosodium glutamate

Wash and drain the rice 1 hour before cooking. Mix with chicken and soup stock. Bring to a boil and cook for 1 hour. Add 2 t. salt, $2/3$ T. soy sauce and monosodium glutamate and cook for 1 more hour. Just before removing from fire, add green onion. Serve while hot. Makes 2 servings.

BENTO, LUNCH BOX LUNCHES

I. **Makunouchi Bento, consisting of the following**

    a. broiled fish
    b. fried pork
    c. fried egg
    d. spinach
    e. white kidney beans
    f. sweet-sour shrimp
    g. chicken and vegetables
    h. pickles
    i. sesame seeds rice

a. Broiled Fish (white fish fillet)

    10 ozs. fish fillet
    salt

Cut into 5 equal pieces. Cover both sides of each piece with salt and let it stand for 2 hours. Rinse quickly and wipe with paper towels to absorb extra moisture. Insert skewers as figured on page 44. Broil on both sides. A charcoal fire is usually used.

Remove the skewers with care so that the fish will not break and allow to cool on a dish.

b. Fried Pork

    1/2 lb. pork
    1 T. *sake*
    1 T. soy sauce
    cornstarch
    frying oil

Cut the pork into oblong pieces about 2 in. long. Mix the *sake* and soy sauce and mix thoroughly with the pork. After 1 hour drain off

89

any excess liquid and coat the meat with cornstarch.   Fry the meat in deep-fat and place it on paper towels to absorb the excess fat.

c. Fried Eggs

3 eggs
2 1/2 T. soup stock (No. 2 or 3)
1 t. soy sauce
a pinch of salt
2 1/2 t. sugar
monosodium glutamate

Beat the eggs with the soup stock, soy sauce, salt, monosodium glutamate and sugar.   Heat and oil a square frying pan.   When hot, pour in half of the egg mixture.   Fry the egg leaving it in one piece.   When the first half is cooked, roll it up toward one side leaving it in the pan while the second half is cooked in the same pan after greasing once more.   When the second half is cooked, roll it up also with the front half so that you have 1 round roll of egg.   When cold, slice into rounds about 1/4 in. thick.

d. Spinach

1 lb. spinach
salt
3 T. soy sauce
1 t. sugar
1 T. white sesame seeds
monosodium glutamate

Boil the spinach in salted boiling water.   Be careful not to overcook.   When tender, drain and dip quickly in cold water.   Drain once more. (In Japan, spinach is sold in packages with the roots all neatly pointing in one direction.   Roots, stem and leaves are all eaten.   When it is served it also is carefully laid out and not mixed up at all.)   This recipe calls for laying the spinach on a plate, in order and pouring over it 1 1/2 T. soy sauce for flavoring.   *Sudare* is made of bamboo to roll food in to make a uniform roll.   A good substitute would be stiff waxed paper.

Placing half of the spinach with root ends to the right on *sudare* and the other half with the root ends to the left, roll the

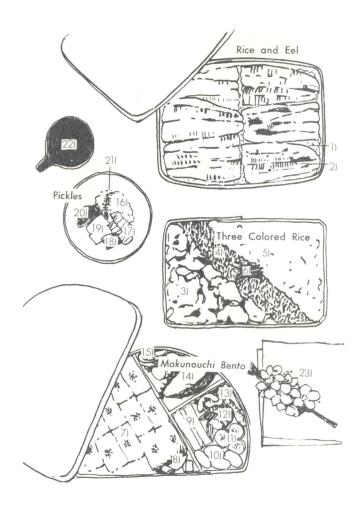

1)	rice	2)	broiled eel
3)	chicken meat	5)	egg
4)	parsley	6)	red pickled ginger
7)	rice shaped *makunouchi*	12)	sweet-sour shrimp
8)	pickle	13)	fried pork
9)	fried egg	14)	broiled fish
10)	sweet boiled white bean	15)	chicken and vegetables
11)	spinach		
16)	cabbage	21)	ear of beefsteak plant
17)	*narazuke* (a kind of pickles)		
18)	red pickled ginger	22)	eel gravy
19)	pickled radish		
20)	cucumber	23)	peach flower

spinach into a uniform roll. Remove from *sudare* and cut the roll into 1¼ in. pieces. Prepare a sauce of 1½ T. soy sauce, 1 t. sugar and a pinch of monosodium glutamate. The spinach rolls are placed in the sauce so that the cut ends of the pieces of roll can absorb the sauce until it is thoroughly flavored. Since they are to be packed into lunch boxes, they can be left standing in the sauce until ready to be packed. After packing, sprinkle parched sesame seeds on the top. (The sesame seeds must be put into a dry skillet and heated until they start to "jump". This is called parching.)

e. White Kidney Beans

> 1 cup white kidney beans
> 1 cup sugar
> salt

Wash and cover the white kidney beans with cold water. Allow to soak for 10 hours or overnight. Simmer the white kidney beans until tender in the same water, but be careful that the white kidney beans are not overcooked (mushy). Add the sugar with ¼ t. salt and continue simmering for 15 minutes. Drain and chill.

f. Sweet-sour Shrimp

> 10 shrimp
> 2 T. vinegar
> ²/₃ t. salt
> 1½ t. sugar
> monosodium glutamate

Devein the shrimp. Cook in salted water with shells on (1 t. salt to 2½ cups of water). Shell the shrimp with the exception of the tail section which is left on to give a natural looking effect. Mix the other ingredients and marinate the shrimp in the sauce for 2 hours.

g. Chicken and Vegetables

> 1 lb. taro*
> ½ lb. chicken meat
> ¼ lb. carrots
> a few dried mushrooms

1/4 lb. bamboo shoots*
2 ozs. string beans
1 square of *konnyaku*
5 ozs. burdock root*
sake
soy sauce
salt
sugar
1 cup soup stock (No. 2 or 3)
mirin

Pare the taro and cut into 1/2 in. cubes. Cook in salted water. Rinse in cold water and drain. Cut each vegetable and *konnyaku* the same as the taro. Cook the *konnyaku* and burdock root in unsalted water.

Cut the chicken into slices and cook in a mixture of 3 T. soy sauce, 2 T. *sake*, 2 T. *mirin* and 1 T. sugar. When tender, drain off excess liquid, saving it for later use. Allow the chicken to cool.

Soften the dried mushrooms in water before cooking. (Dried mushrooms are available all year in Japan, whatever mushrooms are available would be satisfactory, except canned.) Heat 2 T. soy sauce with 2 t. sugar and cook the dried mushrooms in this for several minutes. Drain off the excess liquid saving for later use. Chill, remove the stems and cut the larger mushrooms into 2 or 3 pieces but leave the smaller ones whole.

Mix the sauce which the chicken was cooked in and the other sauce well. Add 1 cup of soup stock, 2/3 t. salt, carrots, bamboo shoots, burdock root, *konnyaku* and taro and cook until flavored. Drain.

String the string beans and boil in salted water (2/3 t. salt to 3 cups of water). Rinse in cold water and drain. Mix the string beans, 1 t. sugar, 1/3 t. salt and monosodium glutamate. Garnish the chicken and vegetables with the string beans.

h and i. Pickles and Sesame Seeds Rice

See page 80 how to cook rice. When the rice is cool, shape it into small rolls with your hands and sprinkle parched black sesame seeds on the top.

Takuwan, *narazuke* and red pickled ginger are usually served as pickles with this. The first two are made from Japanese radish. The ginger is fresh ginger with red coloring added.

A little of each of the foregoing foods are packed into a lunch box, in a pleasing and attractive manner. Usually a lunch box is about 1 in. deep and either a square or round shape about 5–6 in. long.

2. Chicken Rice

1/2 lb. chicken meat
2 eggs
1–2 pieces of red pickled ginger
2 T. green *nori* seaweed
mirin
sake
sugar
salt
soy sauce
monosodium glutamate
4 cups polished rice

Chop the chicken into small pieces. Add 2 T. *mirin*, 1 1/2 T. *sake*, 3 T. soy sauce and 1 T. sugar to the chicken, cook until tender and drain.

Beat the eggs with 1 t. sugar, 1/4 t. salt and a pinch of monosodium glutamate. Heat and oil into a skillet. Fry the egg mixture in as thin as possible sheets using only enough to barely cover the bottom of the pan. This is enough for several sheets. Cut into the shape which will fit the lunch box so that it can be used as a cover for the rice, or cut into interesting shapes that one can easily eat.

Cut red pickled ginger into strips.

Fill lunch box with rice (see "How to cook the rice" page 80). Garnish the rice with chicken and eggs. Add a little of red pickled ginger in the center.

SUSHI, VINEGAR RICE

I. Nigiri Sushi, Sushi Shaped in Oblong Form

    4 cups rice
    1 cuttlefish
    5 shrimp
    1/2 lb. sea bream
    5 ozs. cockles (a salt water mollusk)
    3 sea eel
    3 eggs
    2 sheets of *nori* seaweed
    1/2 lb. fresh tuna fish
    sake
    mirin
    sugar
    soy sauce
    vinegar
    horseradish or *wasabi*
    salt

Cook the rice and season as for *sushi* rice a) page 81.

Remove head, shell and devein the shrimp. Slit the under side, open flat and wash.

Remove the legs from the body of the cuttlefish. Remove 2 layers of thin skin from the body and cut into oblongs ($2^1/3 \times 1^1/2$ in.). Cut the sea bream into pieces the same size as the cuttlefish. Also, cut the tuna fish into the same size chunks. If pieces of tuna fish are left-over, cut them into pieces the size of the little finger. Use canned cockle as is. Use canned eel and prepare in the same size as the cuttle-fish. If the eel is not seasoned, mix 3 T. soy sauce and 1 T. sugar and boil until the liquid evaporates. Spread this on the top side of the eel slices. When putting the eel with the rice make sure the sauce side is on the top. Beat the eggs well, add 1 T. sugar, 1 t. soy sauce, $1/3$ t. salt, $1^1/2$ T. *mirin* and 2 T. soup stock and fry in a square skillet in one piece ($1/3$ in. thick).

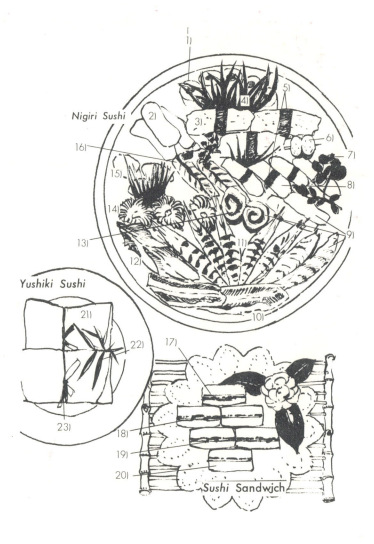

Nigiri Sushi

Yushiki Sushi

Sushi Sandwich

1)	tuna fish	9)	tuna fish
2)	tuna fish	10)	sea-eel
3)	fried egg	11)	shrimp
4)	*haran*	12)	shell fish
5)	*nori* seaweed	13)	rice
6)	ginger	14)	cockle fish
7)	*bofu* leaf	15)	sea urchin
8)	white fish fillet	16)	young konosirus
17)	egg and red pickled ginger	19)	dried mushroom and dried gourd
18)	cucumber and ham	20)	rice
21)	egg	23)	dried gourd
22)	bamboo leaf		

When fried, cut into squares the size of the cuttlefish. If using powdered horseradish, mix with water, if using raw horseradish, grate it.

To make the *sushi*, follow the directions under the figure.

Horseradish is used only with the raw fish (except eel) and not with the egg, etc. Serve cold.

How to make nigiri sushi

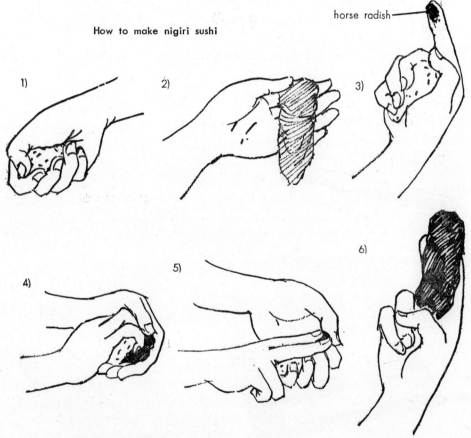

1) In the right hand form the rice ball.
2) In the left hand hold the ingredients to be placed on the top of the rice ball.
3) Holding the rice ball in the right hand, on the forefinger place horseradish.
4) Place the rice ball as shown on the fish with the horseradish between the rice and fish.
5) With the right and middle finger, apply pressure and pick up as shown in 6).

2. Norimaki Sushi

4 cups rice
2 eggs

10 dried mushrooms
1 oz. dried gourd
7 sheets of *nori* seaweed
1 lb. spinach
1 *kamaboko* fish cake
1 oz. red pickled gingers
1^1/$_2$ cups soup stock (No. 2 or 3)
soy sauce
sake
salt
mirin
sugar
monosodium glutamate

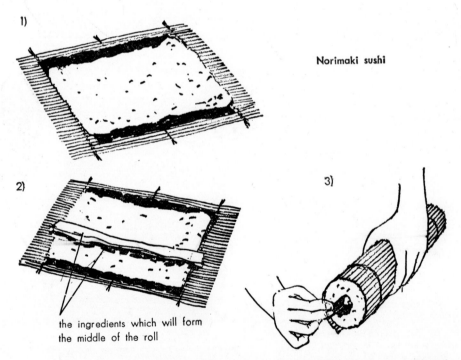

Norimaki sushi

the ingredients which will form the middle of the roll

1) On the top of the bamboo mat, (waxed paper might be a good substitute) lay 1 sheet of seaweed and place rice to the edge of the seaweed on the side, leaving a small area of seaweed open to roll on the top and bottom.
2) Place the ingredients which will form the middle of the roll on the top of the rice from side to side.
3) Using pressure, roll the bamboo mat and ingredients as shown.

96

Cook and season the rice as for *Kansai sushi* b) page 82.

Beat the eggs and add 1 1/2 T. soup stock, 1 t. soy sauce, 1/4 t. salt, 1 1/2 t. sugar and monosodium glutamate. Mix well.

Fry the eggs as directed on page 94 and cut into pieces a little smaller than the little finger. Soften the dried mushrooms in water and season by cooking in 3 T. soup stock, 2 T. soy sauce, 2 T. *sake*, 1 1/2 T. *mirin* and 1 t. sugar. When well seasoned, drain and cut into strips. Save the sauce. Soften the dried gourd in salt water for 30–40 minutes. Bring to a boil in the same water. Using the sauce in which the dried mushrooms were cooked, add 5 T. soup stock, 1/2 t. salt and the dried gourd. Cook until flavored and drain. Cut into lengths as long as the width of the sea-weed. Boil the spinach in salted boiling water until tender, dip in cold water and squeeze the water out. Sprinkle 1 T. soy sauce and mix well. Squeeze once more. Slice the fish cake into rolls 1/2 in. in diameter and as long as the width of the seaweed. Cut the red pickled ginger into tiny, tiny strips. Hold the seaweed over the flame and allow it to be "crisped".

Using a little of each for center ingredients, roll the seaweed as shown. The center ingredients are fish cake, spinach, dried mushrooms, dried gourd and eggs. Cut each roll into 8–9 pieces. Serve cut ends up.

3. Inari no Hosomaki

> 2 cups rice
> 10 squares of fried soy bean curd
> 1/2 oz. dried gourd
> 2 cups soup stock (No. 2 or 3)
> salt
> soy sauce
> sugar
> *sake*
> monosodium glutamate

Prepare the rice for *sushi* b) page 82

Open the fried soy bean curd on 3 sides to lay flat. To remove excess grease, place in a colander the fried side up and pour hot water over it. Mix 1 1/2 cups soup stock, 3 T. soy sauce, 1/2 t. salt, 1 1/2 T. sugar and monosodium glutamate and bring to a boil. Add the fried soy bean curd and when well flavored, remove from sauce and

97

drain. When it is cool, squeeze gently to remove liquid. Soften the dried gourd in salted water, wash and cook until tender. Add the dried gourd to the sauce in which the fried soy bean curd was seasoned. Cook until well flavored. Drain.

Place the fried soy bean curd inside up, on the top of *sudare* (bamboo mat). Place 1/10th of the rice on the fried soy bean curd leaving 3/4 in. of the fried soy bean curd without anything for rolling purposes. On the left and right edge, make the rice slightly higher in thickness. About 1/3 from the bottom of the square of the fried soy bean curd, place 2-3 strings of dried gourd across from left to right and from the bottom roll the entire piece to the top.

Cut 1 roll into 4 pieces, place about 8 pieces on an individual plates and serve.

4. Kazari Sushi, Decorated Sushi

3 cups rice
a) 5 shrimp, 2 small cucumbers
b) 1/2 lb. sliced chicken meat, 10 dried mushrooms, 5 Japanese pepper sprouts or green leaves
c) 4 eggs, 2 t. soy sauce, 1/2 t. salt, 1 T. sugar, 3 T. soup stock (No. 2 or 3), monosodium glutamate, 1 1/3 ozs. white fish fillet, 2/3 oz. red pickled ginger
d) 2 slices of boneless ham, 3 dried prunes
e) 5 slices of canned pineapple, 2 stuffed olives, 5 small shrimp
vinegar
salt
sugar
soy sauce
mirin
sake
monosodium glutamate

Cook and season the rice for *sushi* b) page 82.

When the rice is cool, mold into squares 1/3 in. thick. (In Japan, use the molding box (*oshiwaku*) shown in figure on page 101.)

a) Shell the shrimp except for tail and adjoining segment and devein. Slit the under side and open flat. Mix 2 T. vinegar, 1/2 t. salt, 1 1/2 t. sugar and monosodium glutamate well. Marinate the shrimp until

Chirashi Sushi

Kazari Sushi

1)	dried mushroom	7)	cuttlefish
2)	red pickled ginger	8)	shrimp
3)	Japanese pepper sprout	9)	green peas
4)	lotus root	10)	ground fish fillet
5)	strip of fried egg sheet	11)	bamboo sprout
6)	young konosirus		
12)	pineapple	18)	red pickled ginger
13)	olive		
14)	shrimp	19)	chicken meat
		20)	dried mushroom
15)	cucumber	21)	Japanese pepper sprout
16)	shrimp		
		22)	ham
17)	fried egg	23)	prune

ready to use. Cut both ends of cucumber and slice the cucumber into very thin rounds. Cut a square of rice into smaller squares just a bit larger than 1 shrimp. Make 5 squares, using 1 shrimp and a few cucumbers on the top of each.

   b) Soften the dried mushrooms in water and remove the hard stems. Mix 3 T. soy sauce, 2 T. *sake*, 3 T. *mirin* and $1/2$ T. sugar and bring to a boil and continue cooking until well flavored. Remove from sauce, drain and cut into strips. Add 2 T. *sake*, 1 T. *mirin*, 2 T. soy sauce and 2 t. sugar to the sauce in which the dried mushrooms were cooked and bring to a boil. Place the slices of chicken (without skin) into the sauce and cook until well flavored. Remove from sauce and cool. Cut into strips. In the squares of pressed and molded rice, with a cookie cutter, make 5 heart shapes. Dividing the heart shapes down the center with Japanese pepper sprouts, place chicken on one side and mushrooms on the other side.

   c) Grind the fish fillet and to this add 4 eggs, one at a time and mix well. Add 3 T. soup stock, 2 t. soy sauce, $1/2$ t. salt, 1 T. sugar and monosodium glutamate and mix well. Skim residue that rises to the top. Pour the mixture into a greased 6 in. square pan and place in a low oven for 30 minutes (until set). Remove from the oven, allow to cool, remove from pan and cut into $2^1/3 \times 2^2/3$ in. squares. Cut the pressed rice into equal size. Place 1 piece of the egg on 1 square of rice and garnish with red pickled ginger (which has been cut into fine strips) in the center of the egg. Make 5.

   d) Cut the boneless ham slices into half-moon shapes about the same size as the other squares. (Any pretty cookie cutter shape would be satisfactory.) Cook the prunes in 1 cup of water with 1 T. sugar until soft and allow to cool in the pan. Cut in half and remove the pit. Cut the same shape and size as the ham in the squares of pressed rice. Place the ham on the top and garnish with 2 halves of prunes. Make 5.

   e) Devein the shrimp and drop in boiling salted water. When tender, remove and shell. Trim the ends. Marinate in $1^1/2$ T. vinegar, $1/4$ t. salt, $1/2$ t. sugar and monosodium glutamate until ready to use. Slice the olives. Cut the pressed rice into squares the size of the sliced pineapple, place the pineapple on the top and in the center hole place 1 shrimp and 1 olive. Make 5.

Place all of the sandwiches on a large plate with a lace paper and serve.

5. Sushi Sandwiches

    3 cups rice

    a molding box (*oshiwaku*)

    a) 2 slices of boneless ham, 1 small cucumber, salt, vinegar, mono-sodium glutamate, sugar

    b) $1/3$ oz. dried mushrooms, $1/3$ oz. dried gourd, $1/2$ cup soup stock (No. 2 or 3), *sake*, soy sauce, salt, sugar, monosodium glutamate

    c) 3 eggs, $2^1/2$ T. soup stock (No. 2 or 3), $1/3$ t. salt, 2 t. sugar, 1 t. soy sauce, monosodium glutamate

    d) 1 oz. red pickled ginger

    e) 6 sheets of *nori* seaweed

Cook the rice for *sushi* b) page 82.

Slice the cucumber crosswise $1/8$ in. thick. Salt and allow to stand until soft. Drain and place in a mixture of 2 T. vinegar, $2/3$ t. salt, 2 t. sugar and monosodium glutamate and allow to marinate until ready to use.

Soften the dried mushrooms in cold water. Mix $1^1/2$ T. soup stock, 1 T. soy sauce and $2/3$ T. sugar and bring to a boil. Add the dried mushrooms and continue cooking until well flavored. Remove from the sauce and mince. Add the rest soup stock, $1/2$ t. salt, 2 t. sugar and $1/2$ T. soy sauce to the sauce. Add the dried gourd (preboiled) and cook until well flavored. Remove from the sauce and mince. Mix with the dried mushrooms and gently squeeze the liquid out.

Beat the eggs and add $2^1/2$ T. soup stock, $1/3$ t. salt ,2 t. sugar, 1 t. soy sauce and monosodium glutamate and mix well. For cooking directions, see page 90. When the egg is done, slice across the width of the square about $1/4$ in. thick and diagonally from top to bottom. Slice the red pickled gingers into very fine strips.

Divide the cooked rice into 6 parts. Mold and press half of 1 portion of rice. On the rice, place 1 slice of ham, spread thinly with mustard, place a layer of cucumber on the mustard and place the other half of the rice on the top. Press hard to mold. Remove and wrap in a sheet of *nori* seaweed that has been crisped by holding over a flame for a minute.

Make 1 more ham sandwich. Cut them into 5 or 6 pieces per sandwich. In the same manner, make 2 of dried mushroom and gourd sandwiches by placing between the rice, the minced dried mushroom and gourd and 2 of egg and ginger sandwiches. Serve them on a large plater.

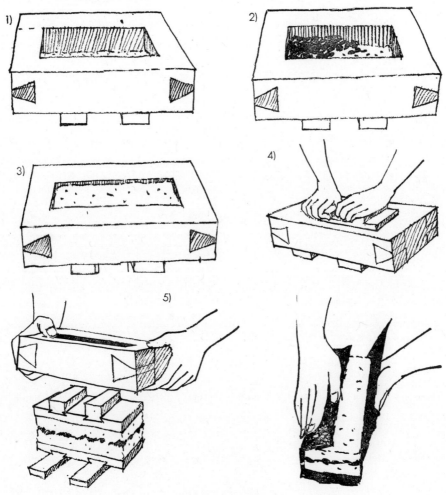

Sushi sandwiches

1) Place half of the rice in the box and level it.
2) Place the ham, horseradish and cucumber on the rice. (Other things are sometimes used instead of ham, etc.)
3) Place the rest of the rice on the top and level it.
4) Place the cover on the top and apply pressure.
5) Remove the outside of the box.
6) Wrap the rice in seaweed as shown.

6. Chirashi Sushi

    4 cups rice
    15 dried mushrooms
    1 egg
    5 T. green peas*
    1 *kamaboko* fish cake
    1 oz. dried gourd
    3 ozs. carrots
    1/2 lb. lotus root
    3 ozs. bamboo shoots*
    3 *konosirus punctatus* fish (Latin)
    5 shrimp
    2/3 oz. red pickled ginger
    soup stock (No. 2 or 3), soy sauce, *sake*, salt, sugar, vinegar, cornstarch,
    mirin

Prepare the rice for *sushi* b) page 82.

Soften the dried mushrooms in water. Remove the stems. Mix 2 1/2 T. *mirin*, 1 1/2 T. *sake*, 3 T. soy sauce and 1 1/2 T. sugar and bring to a boil. Add the dried mushrooms and over a low flame cook until well flavored. Remove from the sauce and drain. Soften the dried gourd in salted water and cook until soft in plain water. Add 5 T. soup stock and 1 t. salt to the sauce in which the dried mushrooms were cooked. Add the dried gourd and cook until well seasoned. Remove from the sauce and gently squeeze the sauce out. Mince. Scrape and julienne (3/4 in. long) the carrots. Add 4 T. soup stock, 1 T. soy sauce, 1 t. salt and 2 t. sugar to the sauce in which the dried gourd was cooked. Add the carrots and cook until well flavored. Remove from the sauce and drain. Cut the bamboo shoots into slices and cook in the sauce from the carrots until the sauce is nearly gone. Peel the lotus root, cut into quarters and slice thinly. Add to 4 cups water, 1 1/2 T. vinegar and lotus root to prevent discoloration. Throw away this water and boil in a new solution, same proportions, of vinegar and water. Drain. Mix well 3 1/2 T. vinegar, 1 1/2 T. salt, 1 1/2 T. sugar and monosodium glutamate and marinate the lotus root for at least 1 hour. Clean and debone the *konosirus punctatus* leaving the 2 side pieces of flesh intact. Salt. Allow to stand for 1 hour. Wash and wipe dry. Marinate in plain vinegar for 1 hour. Cut each side of the *konosirus punctatus* fish body into 5 pieces diagonally. Devein and insert a skewer into the back of the shrimp. Drop into salted boiling water and cook until tender. Shell except for the tail and adjoining section. Slit the under side and open flat. Mix 2 T. vinegar, $2/3$ t. salt, 1 t. sugar and monosodium glutamate and marinate the shrimp for 1 hour.

Beat the egg with $1/6$ t. salt, $1/2$ t. sugar, $1/4$ t. cornstarch dissolved in 1 t. water and monosodium glutamate. Fry in as thin as possible sheets. When cool, cut in strips. Cook the green peas, being careful to retain the color. Cut the fish cake into 2 lengthwise and cut into $1/8$ in. thin slices. Cut the red pickled ginger into fine strips.

Mix the carrots and dried gourd with the rice and divide into 5 individual rice bowls. Arrange the other prepared ingredients in an attractive manner on the top of the rice. Serve warm or cold.

7. Yushiki Sushi, Egg Wrapped Sushi

$2^1/2$ cups rice
3 dried mushrooms
$1/2$ oz. dried gourd
2 ozs. bamboo shoots*
2 ozs. carrots
3 ozs. fresh white fish fillet
5 shrimp
2 T. green peas*
5 eggs
5 Japanese pepper sprouts
$2/3$ oz. red pickled ginger
10 in. edible *konbu* seaweed (if not available, use dried gourd)
mirin, sake, soy sauce, salt, sugar, vinegar, red coloring,
1 cup soup stock (No. 2 or 3), cornstarch

Cook the rice for *sushi* b) page 82.

Soften the dried mushrooms in cold water and remove the stems. Cook until flavored in $1^1/2$ T. soy sauce, $1^1/2$ T. *sake*, 1 T. *mirin* and $1^1/2$ t. sugar. Remove from the sauce and cut into strips. Soften the dried gourd in salt water. Boil until tender in plain water. Cook until flavored in the sauce from the dried mushrooms to which was added 2 T. soup stock, $1/3$ t. salt and $2/3$ t. sugar, squeeze out the liquid from the dried gourd after it is

103

well flavored and cut into strips. If edible *konbu* seaweed is not available, save 5 pieces about 10 in. long to tie the *sushi* with. Cut the bamboo shoots in strips (3/4 in. long). Scrape and julienne the carrots. Cook the bamboo shoots and carrots until tender in the sauce which the dried gourd was cooked. Boil the fish in water until tender. Remove all bones. Grind, cook with 1/3 t. salt, 2/3 t. sugar and monosodium glutamate and mix in red coloring. Cook until all liquid is absorbed, stirring constantly. Prepare the shrimp as in the previous recipe page 103. Cook the green peas being careful not to lose the green color.

Yushiki sushi

1) On the sheet of egg, place rice and other ingredients.
2) Wrap up.
3) Tie with a strip of dried gourd.

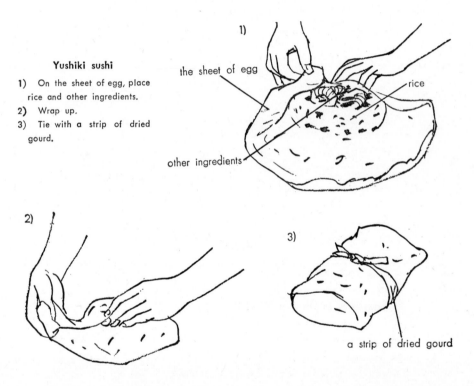

the sheet of egg

rice

other ingredients

a strip of dried gourd

Add to 1 beaten egg 1/8 t. salt, monosodium glutamate and a little (1/5 t.) of cornstarch dissolved in 1/3 T. water. Mix well and fry the eggs one at a time to form round sheets to wrap the *sushi* in.

If using edible *konbu* seaweed, cover in vinegar to soak overnight to soften. Cut in long strings 3/8 in. thick to be used as ties for the *sushi*.

Add to the rice, the dried mushrooms, dried gourd, bamboo shoots

104

and carrots and mix well. Divide into 5 portions. On the fried egg place a heap of rice and put the fish and shrimp on it and garnish with the green peas and a Japanese pepper sprout. The side of the egg which has become browned during frying should be on the inside of the egg roll. Wrap with the egg as shown. Tie with the edible *konbu* seaweed or dried gourd beautifully. Make 5 in the same manner.

Place it with the striped red pickled ginger on an individual plate and serve.

NABE RYORI, FIRE SIDE COOKING

This type of cooking is done at the table and is eaten while still being cooked. One common size pan takes care of 4 or 5 persons.

I. Sukiyaki

1^1/$_2$ lbs. beef, sliced bacon-thin
10 green onions or onions
2 bunches of *shirataki* (long *konnyaku*)
^{2}/$_3$ lb. *shungiku* (edible chrysanthemum leaves) or cabbages
2 squares of broiled soy bean curd
^{2}/$_3$ lb. bamboo shoots*
^{1}/$_3$ lb. carrots
^{2}/$_3$ cup soy sauce
8 T. sugar
2 cups water to make soup stock
10 in. *konbu* seaweed (used for seasoning soup stock only)
^{1}/$_4$ cup soy beans

Mix the water, soy beans and *konbu* seaweed to make the soup stock and allow to stand for about 10 hours. Add ^{2}/$_3$ cup of soy sauce and 8 T. sugar, bring to a boil, remove from fire and strain.
Cut the green onions slantingly into about ^{1}/$_4$ in. lengths. Wash the edible chrysanthemum leaves thoroughly. Drain. Wash and cut the *shirataki* into about 3 in. lengths. Cut the broiled soy bean curd into 12 squares. Slice the carrots into strips of 1^1/$_2$ × ^{1}/$_3$ in. Cut the bamboo shoots into thin slices by cutting crosswise. Arrange the vegetables colorfully on a large plater. See picture.

Put a piece of suet into the skillet, when it is melted, add some of each vegetable starting with those that take the longest to cook and brown them. Add some of the meat on the top of the vegetables and add the soup stock. Last of all, add the *shirataki* and soy bean curd. Do not put in all of the foods at once. Adjust seasoning to taste by adding more soy sauce or sugar. This is to be eaten as it is cooked

106

Ingredients for *Sukiyaki*

1) *shirataki*
2) bamboo shoot
3) carrot
4) broiled soy bean curd
5) beef
6) beef fat (suet)
7) green onion
8) *shungiku* edible
   chrysanthemum leaf
9) egg
10) *wan* Japanese soup bowl
11) sugar
12) egg
13) soy sauce pitcher
14) pickle
15) egg
16) chopstick
17) *wan* Japanese soup bowl
18) *sakazuki* wine cup
19) *choshi* sake holder
20) soup stock

and more food added when there is room in the skillet.

Allow 1 egg per person when serving. Individuals will break and mix the raw egg at the table. Dip the *sukiyaki* in the egg and eat with rice.

2. Mizutaki, Boiled Chicken

5 lbs. chopped young chicken (Ask the meat man to cut this into 1 1/2–2 in. pieces with the bone and skin left intact.)
1 T. grated ginger
3 T. minced green onion
1 cup soup stock (No. 1 or 3)
5 T. soy sauce
1 T. lemon juice
1 T. *mirin* or 1/2 T. sugar
salt
pepper
monosodium glutamate

(In recent times, others have added other vegetables, but I feel that this is detrimental to the flavor of the chicken.)

To make the seasoning sauce, mix the soup stock, soy sauce and *mirin* and bring to a boil. Add the lemon juice after chilling.

Bring 15 cups water to a boil. Drop in all the cleaned chicken. Continue boiling with no lid. Skim off fat and residue. Cover and continue boiling about 1 hour. When the chicken is tender enough to fall apart, remove from heat. Bring the pan and heating unit to the center of the table.

Arrange pile of grated ginger and minced green onion on a plate. Have also on the table, salt, pepper and monosodium glutamate and from these seasonings the individual will adjust his own sauce to taste. When the sauce becomes thin, feel at liberty to spoon in chicken soup and drink or add more seasonings to make new sauce.

3. Joyanabe

(Even if eaten every evening, one doesn't tire of this.)

1 1/3 lbs. pork, sliced bacon-thin

107

2^1/$_4$ lbs. spinach
10 in. *konbu* seaweed (for seasoning soup stock only)
1 green onion
1^1/$_2$ ozs. ginger
1 lemon
soy sauce
sake
monosodium glutamate

Mix 4 cups cold water, 4 T. *sake* and *konbu* seaweed and allow to stand for 3 hours to make soup stock.

Wash and drain the spinach. Arrange in order and place on a large plate with the pork. On another smaller plate, arrange grated ginger and the minced green onion, in a small bowl put the lemon juice and have soy sauce and monosodium glutamate on the table.

Bring the soup stock to a boil, remove the *konbu* seaweed and add the pork and spinach a little at a time. When this is cooked, the individual will add to the lemon juice the seasonings he likes and dipping the pork and spinach into the seasoned lemon juice, eat it. When the lemon juice is nearly gone, add soup stock from the skillet and either drink as is or make new sauce.

4. Nikomi Oden (makes 4-6 servings)

10 large taro*
1 *hanpen* fish cake
6 *ganmodoki* fried soy bean curd and vegetables
1/2 lb. ground chicken meat
3 ozs. carrots
1 square of *konnyaku* (made from a tuberous root)
1 lb. radish
6 shrimp
1 egg
6 *satsuma-age* fried fish cakes with vegetables
10 in. *konbu* seaweed (for seasoning soup stock only)
salt
sugar
sake
soy sauce

Mix 5 cups water, *konbu* seaweed and 3 T. *sake* and allow to stand covered for 3 hours. This is used at the last for boiling everything so should be set aside for awhile.

Slice the radish 1/3 in. thick, peel and boil until tender. Peel the taro and boil in salted water until tender. Rinse and drain. Cut the *konnyaku* into 6 squares, boil, rinse and drain. Cut the fried fish cake into 6 squares. Use the fried soy bean curd with vegetables as is. Slice the carrots 1/4 in. thick and cut the edges to make a flower shape of each round. Mince the leftovers. Mix well the ground chicken, 1 egg, 1 T. minced carrot leftovers, 1/2 T. soy sauce, 1 t. sugar and 1/4 t. salt. Divide into 6 equal portions and form patties. Put the chicken patties into boiling soup stock which is made as follows:

Mix 1 cup water, 2 T. *sake*, 1 1/2 T. soy sauce, 1/4 t. salt and 1/2 T. sugar and bring to a boil.

Add the chicken and bring once more to a boil. Remove from fire. Shell the shrimp except for tail and adjoining segment and devein.

Bring the soup stock that was set aside for 3 hours to a boil, remove the *konbu* seaweed, add 1 T. salt and 2 T. sugar and boil once more. Add *konnyaku*, radish, carrots and taro, then cook covered until well flavored. During this process, the water from the radish and taro will thin the soup. Taste the soup and if it tastes too thin, add soup stock from the chicken. Add all the rest of the ingredients and boil until well flavored. To serve, the individual will take from the pan of stew which will have been put in the center of the table on a heating unit and will serve themselves.

5. Chirinabe, Fish Sukiyaki

1 1/3 lbs. fish; globe fish, file fish, red color sea breams
(They are used chopped with the bones including the head.)
5 green onion.
2 squares of soy bean curd
1/2 lb. *shungiku* (edible chrysanthemum leaves) or cabbages
1 1/2 ozs. gingers
1 lemon
sake
soy sauce
10 in. *konbu* seaweed (used seasoning soup stock only)

109

To make the soup stock, add the *konbu* seaweed and 3 T. *sake* to 5 cups of water and allow to stand for 3 hours.

Clean the fish and using head and tail, cut into 3–5 pieces. Cut the green onions into pieces about 1/2 in. long. Wash the edible chrysanthemum leaves and remove all but the blossom. Cut the soy bean curd into 10 equal squares.

Bring the soup stock to a boil and remove the *konbu* seaweed. Add 1/3 of the fish and continue boiling. While boiling, add little by little the rest of the fish and vegetables. This is to be eaten while cooking on the table. See "*joyanabe*" page 108.

Grate the ginger and slice the lemon to use at the table.

6. Yudofu

5 squares of soy bean curd
3 dried brook trouts or dried shrimp
10 in. *konbu* seaweed
3 T. minced green onion
1 lemon
1/3 oz. *katsuobushi* dried bonito fillet
1 1/2 ozs. ginger, grated
soy sauce

To 5 cups of water, add the dried brook trouts and soak for 1 hour. (If dried trouts is not available, substitute the usual *konbu* seaweed and soak for 3 hours, but the trouts is unusually delicious.)

Put the soup stock with the fish into a saucepan. In Japan, the *yudofu* pan is specially made with a container in the center for heating the 7 T. soy sauce and dried bonito fillet therefore, an aluminum cup set into the center of the pan would be usable.

Bring to a boil, add the cut-into-bite-size soy bean curd and continue boiling until the soy bean curd is heated.

When this is ready to eat, each individual, with a spoon will take from the heated cup of soy sauce and dried bonito fillet and put this mixture on his own small dish. Into this he can add lemon juice and/or grated ginger and/or minced green onion.

Taking the soy bean curd from the central pan, he will dip it into his own sauce and eat. Last of all, the fish will be tender enough to eat

in the same manner. It is permissable to drink the soup stock as soup
in a separate cup.

7. Yasainabe, Vegetables

1 lb. radish
1/4 lb. carrots
2/3 lb. turnips
2/3 lb. taro*
1 square of *konnyaku* (made from a tuberous root)
1 square of broiled soy bean curd
10 in. *konbu* seaweed (used for seasoning soup stock only)
2 green onions or small onion
7 ozs. *chu-miso* paste
sake
sugar
2 1/2 T. white sesame seeds
monosodium glutamate

Allow the *konbu* seaweed to stand in 6 cups water for 4 hours.

Slice the radish into 1/3 in. thick rounds and peel. (Use a potato
peeler before cutting if you wish.) Cut the carrots into 1/4 in. thick
rounds and cut into flower shapes if you wish. Peel the turnips and
cut into pieces the size of a walnut. Peel the taro and boil in salted
water until tender. Rinse and drain. Cube the *konnyaku* into 1/3 in.
squares and soak in cold water to remove the harshness. Cut the green
onions about 1/2 in. in length. Cut the broiled soy bean curd into 6
equal pieces. Add all of these vegetables to the soup stock and boil
until tender.

While the vegetables are cooking, make the *miso* sauce as follows:

Heat the sesame seeds in an ungreased skillet until they "jump"
and grind (a blender is used sometimes). Mix the *miso*, 2 T *sake* and
3 T. sugar and over a low flame continue stirring until some of the
liquid evaporates. Remove from fire and add the sesame seeds.

To serve, the individuals eating will take the vegetables from the
pan, dip them into the *miso* sauce and eat. This also is eaten at the
table.

III

8. Karibayaki

(This cooking requires a sort of grate (wire net) to be heated over charcoal fire brazier.)

1 1/3 lbs. choice grade of beef, sliced bacon-thin
3 ozs. suet
5 green onions or onions
1/2 lb. eggplant
1/2 lb. parsley or celery
2/3 lb. bamboo shoots*
1 lb. *matsutake* mushrooms
1 1/2 lbs. radish
sake
soy sauce
sugar
monosodium glutamate
crushed Japanese pepper

Slice the onions into 1/5 in. lengths. Cut the bamboo shoots into half and then slice 1/6 in. thick. Cut the parsley 2 1/2 in. in length. Slice the eggplant 1/6 in. thick and place in water to prevent discoloration. When ready to serve drain. Tear the mushrooms with the hands into edible pieces. Arrange all of these ingredients on a large plate to place on the table. Add the meat.

Grate the radish and drain the juice and to 1 cup of the radish juice to use, add 1 1/2 T. soy sauce, crushed Japanese pepper and monosodium glutamate.

Make a soup stock of 3 parts of soy sauce, 2 parts of *sake*, 1 part of *mirin* and 2 parts of sugar.

In the center of the table, place in addition to the plate of meat and vegetables a bowl of the soup stock, the heater and skillet with the suet added and a small bowl into which the soy sauce, radish, Japanese pepper sauce has been placed. To cook, take from the plate of uncooked food and dipping it into the soup stock, place it in the heated skillet after the suet has been cooked. When it is tender, take it from the skillet, dip it into the radish sauce and eat.

9. Hakusainabe, Chinese Cabbage

2 lbs. Chinese cabbage or cabbage

Yosenabe

1)	spinach	9)	scallop ligament
2)	chicken meat	10)	carrot
3)	chinese cabbage	11)	egg
4)	*naruto* fish cake	12)	green onion
5)	*harusame*	13)	fish fillet
6)	shrimp	14)	*konbu* seaweed
7)	pork	15)	*sake*
8)	dried mushroom		

$1^1/_2$ lbs. pork, sliced bacon-thin
3 ozs. carrots
$1/_2$ oz. green onions
$1^1/_2$ ozs. ginger, grated
1 lemon
4 cups pork soup stock
soy sauce
monosodium glutamate

Wash and cut the Chinese cabbage into chunks (2 in. long). Cut the carrots into $1/_4$ in. thick rounds and cook until tender. Rinse and drain. Arrange the carrots, Chinese cabbage and pork on a large dish to be placed on the table.

Place on the table the heater and skillet, the plate of food, a plate with a pile of ginger on one side and minced green onions on the other, soy sauce and monosodium glutamate, also a bowl of lemon juice for each person. Place the soup stock in a deep skillet (or sauce pan), bring to a boil and add the pork, Chinese cabbage and carrots. When done, the individuals eating will add to their bowls of lemon juice, ginger, onions, soy sauce and monosodium glutamate, whatever they like and taking food from the central pan, dip it into the lemon juice and eat.

10. Yosenabe, A Little of Everything

$2/_3$ lb. shrimp
$1/_2$ lb. pork, sliced bacon-thin
$1/_2$ lb. chicken meat, sliced bacon-thin
$1/_2$ lb. Chinese cabbage
1 carton of *harusame* noodles
5 ozs. spinach
1 large green onion
15 dried mushrooms
3 ozs. bamboo shoots*
$1/_2$ *naruto* fish cake
3 ozs. carrots
3 eggs
5 scallops
4 cups chicken soup stock

salt

monosodium glutamate

Shell except for tail and adjoining section, devein and slice the underside to open the shrimp flat. Slice the scallops very thin crossgrain. Slice the fish cakes thinly. Fry the *harusame* noodles quickly and drain on absorbent paper. Wash and cut the Chinese cabbage into $1^1/2$ in. lengths. Wash and remove the roots from the spinach. Cut the green onions into $1/8$ in. thick. Slice the bamboo shoots $1/8$ in. thick. Slice the carrots $1/5$ in. thick and boil till tender. Soften the dried mushrooms in cold water and remove the stems. Hard boil the egg and peel. When the egg is cool, slice. Arrange all of these on a large plate to place on the table.

Bring 5 cups of chicken soup stock with 3 t. salt and monosodium glutamate to a boil. Add 1 kind of vegetable at a time, cook well and eat Usually the strong flavored foods are saved toward the last.

COMMON HOME FOODS

1. Scrambled Eggs

    3 eggs
    2 T. *katsuobushi* dried bonito fillet
    1 t. sugar
    1/2 T. soy sauce
    1/8 t. salt
    monosodium glutamate

Beat the eggs well, add the seasonings and pour into a well greased heavy skillet. Stir continuously with chopsticks while cooking and for about 20–30 seconds after removing from fire. Serve while hot.

2. Yoshino Sushi, Okara Soy Bean Curd Leftovers, Vegetables and Fish

    2/3 lb. *okara* soy bean curd leftovers
    2 eggs
    9 ozs. sardines
    2 1/2 ozs. carrots
    1/3 lb. cucumbers
    3 dried mushrooms
    red pickled ginger
    soy sauce
    salt
    sugar
    vinegar
    salad oil
    monosodium glutamate

Wash, remove the entrails, head and bones of the fish, salt and allow to stand for 1 hour. Wash again and wipe dry. Allow to marinate in vinegar for 1 hour. Remove the skin and slice slantingly in a width of 1/4 in.

Mash the soy bean curd leftovers. Into a well greased skillet with 1 1/2 T. salad oil, add the soy bean curd leftovers and brown. Mix in 1 T. soy suace, 1 t. salt, 1 T. sugar and 2 T. vinegar. Cook until flavored and remove from fire. Allow to cool. Add eggs and monosodium glutamate. Cook while stirring continuously.

Cut the cucumbers and carrots in 1 1/2 in. strips, salt and allow to stand until the cucumbers are soft. Squeeze the liquid out gently. Add 1 T. vinegar and gently squeeze again. Soften the dried mushrooms in cold water and cut into strips.

Mix all of the ingredients into the soy bean curd leftovers. Heap on individual plates with red pickled ginger strips and serve while hot.

3. Broiled Eggplants

2 1/4 lbs. eggplants
1 1/2 T. white sesame seeds
1/2 cup brown *miso* paste
1 cup sugar
salad oil
monosodium glutamate

Remove the stem from the eggplants, cut into bite size and soak in water to prevent discoloration. Parch in a skillet and grind the sesame seeds to be combined with the *miso* paste, sugar and monosodium glutamate.

Into a heated skillet, add 2 T. salad oil and brown the eggplants. Cook until tender. Add the *miso* paste. When well flavored, serve hot.

4. Pork with Persimmon Dressing

2/3 lb. persimmons
1/2 lb. bean sprouts
3 ozs. carrots
3 dried mushrooms
1/2 lb. pork meat
vinegar
salt
sugar
monosodium glutamate

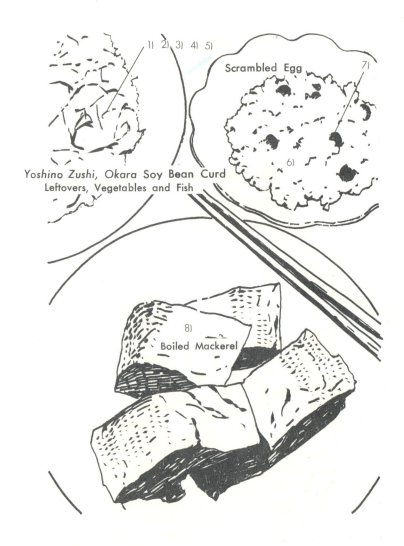

Yoshino Zushi, Okara Soy Bean Curd
Leftovers, Vegetables and Fish

Scrambled Egg

Boiled Mackerel

1) okara soy bean curd leftover
2) carrot
3) dried mushroom

4) fish fillet
5) cucumber

6) egg

7) green peas

8) mackerel

Cook the bean sprouts until tender and drain. Cut the carrots into strips (1^1/2 in. in length), salt and allow to stand until softened. Squeeze out excess liquid. When the dried mushrooms are softened in water, cut in the same manner. To the above vegetables, add 1 T. vinegar, mix well and drain off liquid.

Cut the pork into 2 in. thick slices and salt. Drop into boiling water and cook until tender.

Peel and remove the seeds of the persimmon, grate the fruit in a bowl, mix in 3 T. vinegar, 1 t. salt, ^{2}/3 T. sugar and monosodium glutamate. Mix all together and serve.

5. Zazen Mame, Hard Boiled Soy Beans

    1 cup soy beans
    4 T. soy sauce
    3 T. crude or black sugar (from which molasses is made, or try other
        sugar if this is not available)

Wash and soak the soy beans in water for 10 hours. Bring to a boil and boil for 5-6 minutes. Mix 4 T. soy sauce and 2 T. sugar and continue simmering over a very low flame. When the liquid is nearly gone, mix in the rest of the sugar and continue stirring. (Don't be impatient.) Serve.

6. Irotsukedofu, Egg Dressed Soy Bean Curd

    3 squares of soy bean curd
    1^1/3 cups shaving of *katsuobushi* dried bonito fillet
    3 eggs
    5 T. soy sauce
    3 T. *mirin*
    2 t. sugar

Cut the soy bean curd into 1^1/3 in. cubes. Bring the soy sauce, *mirin* sugar and dried bonito fillet to a boil. When *mirin* smell is gone, add the soy bean curd and continue cooking with cover. Don't overcook.

Beat the eggs well and pour over the soy bean curd. Place the cover on. Cook over a medium fire until the eggs are set, remove from fire and serve. Garnish with minced spring onion or crushed Japanese pepper.

7. Beef and Burdock

$1/3$ lb. round steak beef, sliced bacon-thin
$1/3$ lb. flank from beef, sliced bacon-thin
8 ozs. burdock root*
$2/3$ oz. ginger
soy sauce
sugar

Remove the outer skin of the burdock root and cut into slanted ovals $1/4$ in. thick. Soak in 3 cups water with 1 T. vinegar for about 30 minutes. Rinse and add to 4 cups water. Cook covered for 30 minutes until tender. Add the beef, sliced ginger, 4 T. soy sauce and $2^1/2$ T. sugar and cook for 2 hours covered over a low flame. Serve.

8. Fried Pork and Apple Balls

1 lb. ground pork
3 dried mushrooms
$1/2$ apple
1 egg
$1/4$ green onion or onion
1 lettuce
mustard
sake
salt
vinegar
monosodium glutamate
salad oil
soy sauce

Soften the dried mushrooms in cold water and cut $1/6$ in. cubes. Peel and cut the apple like the dried mushrooms. Mince the onion. Mix all together and add 1 egg, $2/3$ T. *sake*, 1 t. salt and monosodium glutamate. Mix well and make about 15 patties. Fry in deep-fat.

Place on lettuce leaves to serve with a side dish of equal parts of soy sauce and vinegar with monosodium glutamate. Add a bit of mustard.

9. Cabbage and Ham Salad

1³/₄ lbs. cabbage
3 slices boneless ham
3 T. white sesame seeds
vinegar
soy sauce
salt
sugar
monosodium glutamate

Shred the cabbage as fine as possible. In a covered sauce pan, cook until tender, mixing lightly with a fork 2–3 times. Drain and cool.

Shred the ham. Parch and grind the sesame seeds, add 4 T. vinegar, 1 t. salt, 1¹/₂ T. sugar, 1 t. soy sauce and monosodium glutamate. Add the cabbage and ham and mix well.

10. Boiled Mackerel

1¹/₃ lbs. mackerel
2 ozs. rice bran (made from the brown coating of brown rice)
soy sauce
sugar
sake
mirin

Wash the mackerel, remove the entrails, bones, head and tail and cut into 6 pieces.

Mix 4 T. soy sauce, 2¹/₂ T. *sake*, 4 T. *mirin* and 1¹/₂ T. sugar, bring to a boil and add the mackerel. Place a small cover directly on the top of the fish and cover with the regular pan cover also. When the mixture boils and pushes the inner lid up, remove the regular cover. Cook for 2–3 minutes with the smaller one   Then remove the smaller cover replacing the regular cover, turn the flame very low and continue cooking until the sauce is about half of the original volume. Add the rice bran and continue cooking until all of the sauce is absorbed.

Serve as picture.

MENRUI RYORI, VERMICELLI

This cooking is mainly with Chinese noodles or spaghetti in a soup.

I. Gu Somen, Vermicelli with Chicken and Vegetables

1/2 lb. *shirataki somen* (a kind of vermicelli)
1/2 lb. thin sliced chicken meat
1/2 oz. dried mushrooms
1/2 lb. *shungiku* chrysanthemum leaves
1/4 lb. carrots
1 egg
5 cups soup stock (No. 3)
salt
soy sauce
sugar
monosodium glutamate

Drop the vermicelli in boiling water and cook until tender. Rinse in cold water and drain.

Mix 1 1/2 T. soy sauce, 1/2 t. salt, 2 t. sugar, 3 T. soup stock and monosodium glutamate and bring to a boil. Add the thinly sliced chicken and boil till well seasoned.

Mix 5 cups soup stock, 1/2 T. soy sauce, 2 t. salt and monosodium glutamate and set aside until ready to serve.

Wash the edible chrysanthemum leaves and drop in boiling water until tender. Rinse in cold water and drain. Cut in 1 1/2 in. lengths. Cut the carrots and dried mushrooms into strips after softening in cold water. Take enough soup stock to boil the carrots and dried mushrooms until tender. Beat the egg and add a little of salt and monosodium glutamate. Fry in sheets as thin as possible. Cut into strips.

Heat the soup stock to boiling, remove from fire and add the vermicelli. In a large rice bowl with cover, place the vermicelli and arrange the chicken, vegetables and eggs in an attractive manner on the top. Pour hot soup stock over all and serve.

120

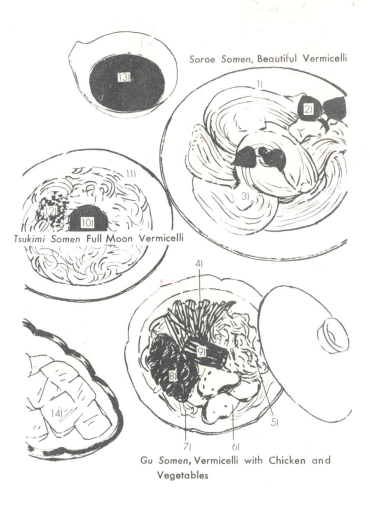

Soroe Somen, Beautiful Vermicelli

Tsukimi Somen Full Moon Vermicelli

Gu Somen, Vermicelli with Chicken and
Vegetables

1)	somen vermicelli	3)	ice
2)	beefsteak plant		
4)	carrot	7)	somen vermicelli
5)	egg	8)	dried mushroom
6)	chicken meat	9)	shungiku edible
			chrysanthemum leaf
10)	egg yolk		
11)	somen vermicelli	13)	sauce
12)	green onion	14)	ice

2. Tsukimi Somen, Full Moon Vermicelli

2/3 lb. *shirataki somen* (a variety of vermicelli)
5 egg yolks
5 *zingiber mioga* flowers (edible)
cracked ice
1 1/2 cups soup stock (No. 4)
soy sauce
sugar
monosodium glutamate

Cook vermicelli until tender in boiling water. Rinse in cold water, drain and chill. Cut the flowers into slices. Mix 1 1/2 cups soup stock, 4 T. soy sauce, 1 1/2 T. sugar and monosodium glutamate and bring to a boil. Remove from fire and chill.

Place vermicelli in a soup bowl, on the top of it place 1 unbroken, uncooked egg yolk with *zingiber mioga* flowers beside it. Pour the soup stock over all and serve cold.

3. Soroe Somen, Beautiful Vermicelli

2/3 lb. *somen* (a variety of vermicelli)
5 *zingiber mioga* flowers, sliced
5 beefsteak plants or green leaves
1 1/2 cups soup stock (No. 4)
soy sauce
sugar
monosodium glutamate
ice

Tie the vermicelli as shown in figure (page 122) and cook until tender in boiling water. Rinse in cold water, drain and chill. Mix 1 1/2 cups soup stock, 4 T. soy sauce, 2 T. sugar and monosodium glutamate and bring to a boil. Remove from fire and chill.

Arrange the vermicelli on a board, straightening out the pieces, cut off the end with the string and divide into 5 equal portions. Place these portions in soup bowls still arranged together. (They may be curled about but all in the same direction.) Place ice, beefsteak plants and sliced flowers on the top. Place soup stock in small individual bowls and serve together. (To eat, put a little vermicelli at a time into the soup stock and eat.)

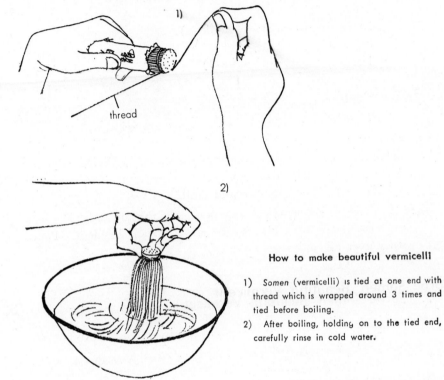

How to make beautiful vermicelli

1) *Somen* (vermicelli) is tied at one end with thread which is wrapped around 3 times and tied before boiling.

2) After boiling, holding on to the tied end, carefully rinse in cold water.

4. Kishimen

   1 lb. *udon* uncooked spaghetti
   5 squares of fried soy bean curd
   1 green onion
   5 cups soup stock (No. 4 or 5)
   soy sauce
   sake
   sugar
   salt
   monosodium glutamate

Boil the spaghetti, rinse and drain.

To remove the excess grease from the fried soy bean curd, pour hot water over it in a colander. Cut it in half. Mix 1/2 cup soup stock, 1 T. *sake*, 2 T. soy sauce and 1 T. sugar and bring to a boil. Add the fried soy bean curd and cook until well flavored. Remove from the soup stock and drain. Cut the green onion diagonally into 1 1/2 in. lengths.

Bring 4 1/2 cups soup stock to a boil, add 1 1/2 T. soy sauce, 1 1/2 t. salt and monosodium glutamate and bring to a boil once more. Remove from heat. Add the spaghetti to the soup stock, cover and allow to warm through. Place the spaghetti without soup stock in individual dishes, place on the top, 2 fried soy bean curd halves and a few spring onion pieces. Pour the soup stock over all gently, cover and serve.

5. Odamaki-mushi, Egg Custard Spaghetti

> 1 lb. *udon* uncooked spaghetti
> 1/3 lb. thin sliced chicken meat
> 1/2 *kamaboko* fish cake
> 1 green onion
> 2 eggs
> 4 cups soup stock (No. 3)
> salt
> soy sauce
> monosodium glutamate

Boil the spaghetti until tender, rinse and drain. Divide into 5 equal portions and place in individual soup bowls. Sprinkle a little soy sauce over the chicken and allow to stand. Cut the fish cake into half and then slice 1/6 in. thick. Slice the green onion diagonally into 1 1/2 in. lengths. (Sliced bamboo shoots and string beans can also be used, if desired.)

Mix 4 cups soup stock, 1/2 T. soy sauce, 1 1/2 t. salt and monosodium glutamate and chill. Beat the eggs and add to the soup stock. Mix well.

Place the other ingredients on the spaghetti in an attractive manner. Pour the egg soup over all and steam until the eggs are set. Serve while hot.

6. Yamakake Soba-mushi

6 ozs. *chasoba* Japanese noodles
1/2 lb. *yamaimo* (Japanese yam)
2 egg whites
5 egg yolks
1 green onion
soup stock (No. 3)
salt
soy sauce
monosodium glutamate

Drop the noodles into boiling water. Stir once or twice to prevent sticking together. When tender, rinse and drain.

Peel *yamaimo* and grate. Mix well in blender with 2 egg whites 2/3 t. salt and monosodium glutamate. Mince the green onion and place in water for a few minutes. Just before using, drain.

Mix 2 1/2 cups soup stock, 1 t. salt, 1 t. soy sauce and monosodium glutamate. Into individual bowls, place the noodles, cover with the *yamaimo* mixture and in a hollow in the middle, place 1 egg yolk. Steam until the egg yolk is partly cooked. Sprinkle with green onion pieces, pour hot soup stock over all and serve with covered.

7. Dango-jiru

1/2 lb. soft wheat flour
1/2 lb. taro*
1/3 lb. radish
1 green onion
3 ozs. carrots
soy sauce
5 cups soup stock (No. 5)
salt
monosodium glutamate

Peel the taro and cut into bite size. Boil in salted water until tender. Rinse in cold water and drain. Peel the radish and carrots and cut into bite size. Cut the green onion into 1/3 in. lengths. Sift the flour, add 6 T. hot water and mix well.

124

Add the vegetables to 5 cups of soup stock and cook until tender. Add 2^1/$_2$ t. soy sauce, 2 t. salt and monosodium glutamate. Drop the dough by the spoonful into the soup and cook until the dough is done. Depending on the season of the year use other vegetables such as Chinese cabbage, eggplant and squash. Serve while hot.

DESSERTS

To Be Made at Home

1. Mizuyokan, Red Bean Kanten

$3/5$ cup *azuki-sarashian* red bean powder
$1^1/2$ cups sugar
$2/3$ *kanten* agar-agar
2 cups water

Dissolve the red bean powder in 1 cup water.

Using *kanten*, break it up and add only enough water to cover. When the *kanten* is soft, squeeze gently to remove the liquid, add to 1 cup water and cook until melted. Add the sugar and stir until dissolved. Simmer until the sugar is dissolved and skim the residue which rises. Add the hot mixture to the red bean powder mixture gradually while stirring. Bring to a boil and skim once more.

Pour into a square cake pan and allow to cool. Remove and cut into 12–16 squares. Wrap in a cherry leaf and serve.

To make *azuki-an* red bean paste from red beans instead of from the red bean powder, $2/3$ cup of red beans makes 1 cup of *azuki-koshian* strained red bean juice. Boil the red beans until they are soft, put them through a food mill, or press through a sieve. Squeeze the juice out through a cheesecloth. This makes 1 cup of juice.

2. Ohagimochi, Red Bean Paste Coated Rice

1 cup *mochi* rice (glutinous rice)
$3/5$ cup *azuki-sarashian* red bean powder
1 cup water
sugar
$1/2$ T. karo syrup
$1/6$ t. salt
2 t. poppy seeds

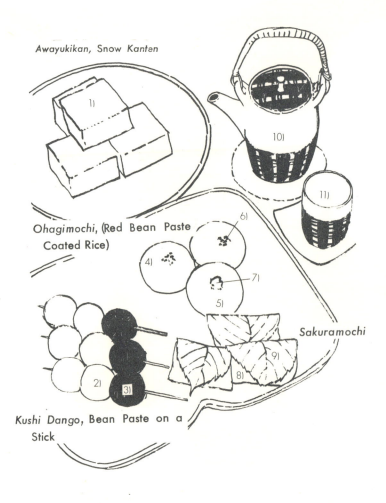

Awayukikan, Snow Kanten

Ohagimochi, (Red Bean Paste Coated Rice)

Sakuramochi

Kushi Dango, Bean Paste on a Stick

1)	*kanten*		sugar
	egg white		
2)	*shiratama* powder	3)	red bean paste
4)	*mochi* rice inside and red bean paste outside	6)	poppy seed
		7)	suger
5)	*mochi* rice inside and soy bean powder outside		
8)	*shiratama* powder and wheat flour	10)	tea pot
9)	salted cherry leaf	11)	tea cup

Dissolve 1/4 cup red bean powder in 2/5 cup water, 1 1/2 cups sugar, 1/2 T. karo syrup and 1/6 t. salt and mix well. Stirring constantly, cook over a low flame until it is the consistency of paste. Wash the rice and soak overnight. Drain. Add 3/4 cup water (If not possible to soak the rice overnight, use the same amount of water as rice.) and cook as directed on page 80. When the rice is taken off the fire, add 4 T. sugar, mix very well, cover and allow to steam. When lukewarm, make balls of rice 1 1/5 in. in diameter. Put enough the red bean paste on a piece of damp cheesecloth to coat the rice, place the rice ball in the center, gather the cloth together and carefully cover the rice ball with the red bean paste. Remove from cloth, sprinkle the poppy seeds over the top. To serve, serve either on a small plate or on a piece of white birch bark, or a pretty leaf.

3. Kinakomochi, Soy Bean Powder Coated Rice

> 5 T. soy bean powder
> 1/4 t. salt
> 4 T. sugar
> 3/5 cup *azuki-sarashian* red bean powder
> sugar
> 1/2 T. karo syrup
> 1/6 t. salt
> 1 cup *mochi* rice (glutinous rice)
> 1 cup water

Make exactly the same as the previous recipe. When the red bean paste coat has been put on, add an outer coating made of 5 T. soy bean powder, 4 T. sugar and 1/4 t. salt. On the top in the center, sprinkle a little sugar. Serve.

4. Awayukikan, Snow Jello

> 2 egg whites
> 1 *kanten* agar-agar
> 2 cups water
> 2 cups sugar
> lemon essence or juice

Prepare *kanten* with water and sugar in a similar manner as was done on page 126. Continue cooking until the mixture reaches the soft ball stage. Remove from fire and cool to about 95° F while stirring. While *kanten* is cooking, stiffly beat 2 egg whites into a square cake pan, pour *kanten* into the stiffly beaten egg whites while stirring. At the same time, add the lemon juice or essence. When cooled cut into 10–12 pieces. Serve.

5. Sakuramochi

> 1 cup soft wheat flour
> 1/6 cup *shiratama* powder
> 20 salted cherry leaves
> 1/2 cup *azuki-sarashian* red bean powder
> 1 cup sugar
> salad oil
> red coloring

Dissolve the red bean powder in 2/3 cup water, add 1 cup sugar and boil until thickened. When it is cool, form 20 balls. Dissolve the *shiratama* powder in 1/2 cup water, add the wheat flour, 1/2 T. sugar and 1/2 cup water and mix well. Add red coloring. Into a greased heated skillet, fry the batter in very thin 4 × 2 1/3 in. pancakes over a low flame. After turning, fry only a short time, put a ball of red bean paste on one half and fold the other half over. Remove from pan. Make 20. Wrap in cherry leaves. Serve.

6. Kushi Dango, Bean Paste on a Stick

> 1/3 cup *shiratama* powder
> 10 toothpicks (4 in. long)
> a) 2/5 cup *azuki-sarashian* red bean powder
> 1 cup sugar
> b) 1/2 cup white kidney beans
> 1 cup sugar
> c) 3 T. soy bean powder
> 2 T. sugar
> salt

Into the *shiratama* powder, add a little water and allow to stand until all is wet. While gradually adding hot water until it becomes doughy, knead with the fingers. Break apart with the fingers and steam.

While still hot, crush into fine particles. With damp hands form 30 balls.

Mix a) ingredients and over a low flame cook until it forms red bean paste. Cool. Coat 10 balls.

Boil the white kidney beans until soft and grind. Add sugar and boil until it forms white bean paste. Coat 10 balls.

Mix c) ingredients, coat 10 balls.

On a long toothpick, place 1 ball of each color with the lighter colored one in the center.

7. Chestnut Sweets

10 chestnuts
$1/2$ cup sugar
$3/5$ cup *azuki-sarashian* red bean powder
$1^1/5$ cups sugar
$1/2$ T. karo syrup
$1/2$ cup cornstarch

Soak the chestnuts overnight in water. Peel and again soak for 2–3 hours in water. Add $1^1/2$ cups water and boil until tender. Add $2/3$ cup sugar and boil until flavored. If possible, allow to stand in this solution overnight. If in a hurry, it is not absolutely necessary. If using canned chestnuts, no cooking or standing is necessary.

Dissolve the red bean powder in 1 cup of water. Add $1^1/5$ cups sugar, $1/2$ T. karo syrup and a little salt and while stirring constantly cook until it thickens to a stiff paste. Cool.

Sift the cornstarch and after forming balls of red bean paste with 1 chestnut inside of each, roll them in the cornstarch and steam until the cornstarch becomes translucent. In order to steam without having the balls stick to the pan, place a damp cloth on the rack and place the sweets on the cloth. Remove after steaming and cool very quickly by fanning.

NEW YEAR'S DAY FESTIVAL DISHES

Zyuzume Ryori, Nest of Boxes Meal

The first meal of the new year is one of great celebration, celebrated by the whole family eating together, a meal which is served only once a year. The menu is the same from year to year and from family to family. It varies only in the amount. There are always 4 tiers in the box and 3, 5, or 7 kinds of food are put in each tier. A certain amount of each kind of food is prescribed so that as the kinds of food increase, the entire amount of food increases. Thankfulness and joy that the new year has come and health for all in the coming year are symbolized in the food.

Each tier of the box has in it only the food which for ages had been the custom. In recent times the younger generation has tended to add foods from other countries, but I would like to see only the Japanese food preserved as a tradition. In this picture are the foods as prescribed by age old customs from the top, number 1, to the bottom, number 4. In the first tier are *kuchitori* special occasion side dishes which are beautiful and very sweet. In the second tier various broiled fish are the center of interest. In the third tier *osechi* boiled vegetables is the center of the tray and in the fourth tier *sunomono* salads are the center of interest. The food is all to be prepared on the preceding day making it possible for the wife's work to be lightened on the most important holiday of the year when everyone rests from work. This tiered box of food is eaten at breakfast and if there are leftovers they can be eaten at later meals. In setting the table for the meal at which the box of food is to be eaten, each person must have 4 dishes to correspond with the 4 tiers of the box. When taking food from the tiers, one must take one of each kind of food. *Otoso* (a special rice wine) is served with the meal.

The Contents of the 4 Tiers

I. Kuchitori, Special Occasion Side Dishes—1st box

a. nishoku yokan, two-colored kanten

New Year's Day Festival Dishes

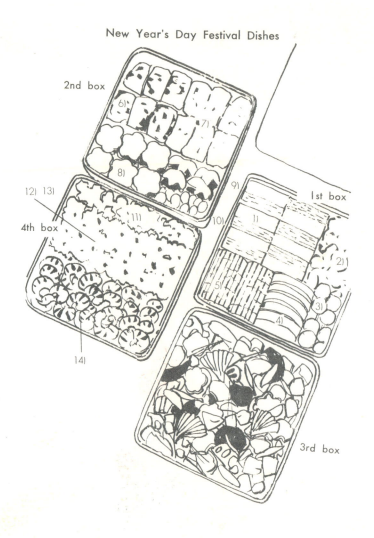

1) *nishoku yokan*, two colored *kanten*   4) *hinode kamaboko*, sunrise fish cake

2) *azuki kinton*, sweet red bean paste   5) *datemaki tamago*, rolled egg

3) *magatama dango*, chicken ball

6) broiled yellow fish with sauce   9) *wakataketo*, bamboo leaf candy

7) flounder with egg sauce   10) *matsuba ginnan* gingko nuts

8) flower shaped egg

osechi-3rd box

burdock	radish
konnyaku	bamboo shoot
broiled soy bean curd	taro
lotus root	*tazukuri* dried young sardine
string bean	carrot
dried mushroom	pine needle

11) chrysanthemum leaf   13) lemon

12) chrysanthemum shaped turnip   14) vinegared shrimp

b. datemaki tamago, rolled egg
c. hinode kamaboko, sunrise fish cake
d. azuki kinton, sweet red bean paste
e. magatama dango, chicken balls

2. Broiled Dishes—2nd box

a. broiled yellowfish with sauce
b. flounder with egg sauce
c. flower shaped egg
d. wakataketo, bamboo leaf candy
e. matsuba ginnan, gingko nuts

3. Osechi, Boiled Food—3rd box

osechi, vegetables without meat or fish flavor

4. Sunomono, Salads—4th box

a. chrysanthemum shaped turnips
b. vinegared shrimp

I. Kuchitori, Special Occasion Side Dishes—I st box (10 servings)

a. Nishoku Yokan, Two-colored Kanten

5/6 lb. *yamaimo* (Japanese yam) or potatoes
1 *kanten* agar-agar
2 cups water
1 cup sugar
salt
vinegar
blue coloring

Peel and cube the *yamaimo*. Add 1 T. vinegar to 4 cups water and soak the *yamaimo* for 30 minutes. In fresh water, boil until tender, drain and mash.

Place the *kanten* in water until soft, squeeze the water out, break into pieces, put into 2 cups water and heat until it melts. Continue

131

cooking and add the sugar. Skim as residue rises. When there is no more residue, remove from fire and add the *yamaimo* mixture. Strain. Bring to a boil again and continue boiling until the mixture is about 2^1/2 cups in volume. Divide in 2. Pour a half into a 5 in. square box to cool and set. Into the other half, add blue coloring. Keep the blue mixture from jelling by placing over hot water until the first half has jelled. Pour hot water over the top of the first half and drain off quickly 2–3 times to melt the top just slightly. Wipe damp-dry with a cloth and then pour the second half of the gelatin mixture over the first half and cool quickly. Remove from the pan and cut into small squares to fill ^{1}/5 of the top box.

b. Datemaki Tamago, Rolled Egg

>5 eggs
>1 ^{1}/3–2 ozs. white fish fillet
>4 T. soup stock (No. 3)
>1 t. soy sauce
>^{1}/2 t. salt
>1 T. sugar
>monosodium glutamate

Grind the fish well, removing the bones and skin. Break the egg into the fish and mix well. Add the soup stock, soy sauce, salt, sugar and monosodium glutamate and mix well. Put through a food mill. Pour the mixture into a greased square cake pan that has been warmed and place in a low oven for 40 minutes. When it is cooked, remove immediately from the pan, place on a bamboo mat and roll. Tie the roll with thread and allow to stand until cool. Remove the bamboo mat and slice ^{1}/3 in. thick.

c. Hinode Kamaboko, Sunrise Fish Cake

>1 large *beni kamaboko* fish cake

Remove from the paper or cardboard to which it is attached and slice ^{1}/3 in. in thickness.

d. Azuki Kinton, Sweet Red Bean Paste

>1. 1 cup white kidney beans
>1^1/2 cups sugar
>^{1}/3 t. salt

2. $3/5$ cup *azuki-sarashian* red bean powder
    1 cup water
    $1^1/5$ cups sugar
    $1/3$ t. salt
    $4/5$ T. karo syrup

Wash and soak the white kidney beans overnight. Over a low flame boil until tender without mashing if possible. Add the sugar and salt and boil for about 10 minutes. Remove from fire and cool. Drain the white kidney beans. Cook the liquid until the half has evaporated. Add the white kidney beans and bring once more to a boil, remove from fire, cool and drain.

Dissolve the red bean powder in 1 cup of water, add sugar, salt, karo syrup and the liquid in which the white kidney beans were cooked.

Over a low flame, stirring constantly, boil the red bean mixture until it is about the consistency of paste. Remove from fire, add the white kidney beans, place on a plate and fan quickly to cool. Place in the box in the form in which it cools.

e. **Magatama Dango, Chicken Balls**

    $1/2$ lb. ground chicken meat
    3 dried mushrooms
    $2/3$ oz. green onion, minced
    $2/3$ oz. carrots
    $4/5$ T. *sake*
    $4/5$ T. soy sauce
    $4/5$ t. sugar
    $1/2$ t. salt
    $1/2$ egg
    monosodium glutamate
    2 T. green *nori* seaweed
    frying oil
    toothpicks

Soften the dried mushrooms in cold water. Drain and mince. Boil the carrots, drain and mince. Add the carrots, mushrooms, onions, soy sauce, *sake*, sugar, egg, salt and monosodium glutamate to the chicken and mix well. Form balls about $3/4$ in. in diameter and fry. When cool, put 2 balls a toothpick and just before placing into the box, sprinkle broken green *nori* seaweed on the balls.

133

2. Broiled Dishes— 2nd box

a. Broiled Yellowfish with Sauce

    1¹/3 lb. yellowfish fillet
    6 T. *mirin*
    4 T. soy sauce
    poppy seeds

If the fish is not cut up, remove the entrails and bones, cut into 2¹/3 × 1¹/3 in. squares and ²/3 in. thick. Mix the *mirin* and soy sauce and marinate the fish in this for 3 hours turning occasionally. Broil as shown on page 44. While still hot remove skewers. Boil the *mirin* and soy sauce until it is about ¹/2 evaporated, spread the sauce on the fish and sprinkle poppy seeds on the top of the sauce. Place in the second box.

b. Flounder with Egg Sauce

    1¹/3 lbs. flounder fillet
    salt
    ⁴/5 cup *mirin*
    1 egg yolk
    monosodium glutamate

Cut the flounder fillet into about 2¹/3 × 1¹/3 in. squares and ²/3 in. thick. Salt and allow to stand for 30 minutes. Rinse and wipe dry. Allow to stand in ⁴/5 cup *mirin* for 1 hour. Mix 1 egg, ¹/3 t. salt and monosodium glutamate, insert skewers as shown on page 44 and broil. When one side is broiled, turn and broil the underside until the egg yolk dries. Remove skewers while still hot. When cool, place in the box.

c. Flower Shaped Egg

    5 eggs
    salt
    sugar
    monosodium glutamate
    red coloring

Hard boil the eggs and while still hot, remove the shells and separate the whites and yolks. Mash the whites and the yolks separately. Mix ¹/4 t. salt, ⁴/5 t. sugar, monosodium glutamate and the mashed egg whites well. Mix ¹/3 t. salt, 1¹/2 t. sugar and monosodium glutamate and the egg yolks well. Spread out a well wrung out damp cheesecloth (5 × 6 1/2 in.). On the top of this place the egg white mixture and with the hands flatten until it covers the cloth. In the center third from top to bottom, place the egg yolks from side to side and roll the cloth with the egg whites around the egg yolks. Place 5 chopsticks (substitute pencils) at equal distances around the roll on the outside of the cloth and tie with thread in several spots. Steam for 10 minutes. When cool, remove the cheesecloth and slice 1/3 in. thick. Place in the box with the sliced side up. (If red "flowers" are desired, add red food coloring to the egg white mixture before rolling.)

d. Wakataketo, Bamboo Leaf Candy

1 *kanten* agar-agar
2 1/2 cups water
3/4 cup sugar
blue coloring

Soften the *kanten* in water. Squeeze the liquid out and tear into small pieces. Add to 2 1/2 cups water and heat until dissolved. Add the sugar and continue cooking until all of the residue that rises has been skimmed and the entire mixture has evaporated to 2/3 of the original volume. Strain. Add blue coloring to make a natural looking leaf color. Pour into a square cake pan and allow to cool. When it is set, remove and cut into desired shapes.

e. Matsuba Ginnan, Gingko Nuts

40 gingko nuts
salt
sugar
monosodium glutamate
15 pairs of pine needles

Remove the hard shells from the nuts, add the nuts to 1/2 cup water and while they are boiling, rub with a spoon to remove the thin skin from the nut. Drain, add cold water to cool and drain again. Mix 1/3 t. salt, 2/3 t. sugar and monosodium glutamate well and add the nuts. Gently stir until the nuts are well covered. Holding a pair of pine needles which are still fastened together at one end, push the needles carefully through 2 nuts. Place in box as shown in the picture.

3. Osechi, Boiled Food —3rd box

1^{1}/$_{3}$ ozs. *tazukuri* dried young sardines
^{3}/$_{4}$ lb. radish
^{1}/$_{4}$ lb. carrots
^{1}/$_{2}$ lb. taro*
^{1}/$_{3}$ lb. lotus root
^{1}/$_{3}$ lb. burdock root*
^{1}/$_{3}$ lb. bamboo shoots*
1 square of *konnyaku* (made from tuberous root)
1 square of broiled soy bean curd
^{2}/$_{3}$ oz. string beans
10 dried mushrooms
7 pairs of pine needles
sake
soy sauce
mirin
salt
sugar
monosodium glutamate

Wash the dried young sardines and add 4 cups of water and ^{4}/$_{5}$ T. *sake* and allow to stand for 5–6 hours. Strain. The liquid is used as soup stock.

Slice the radish ^{1}/$_{3}$ in. thick and cut each of these in thirds to form fan shapes. Slice the carrots ^{1}/$_{5}$ in. thick and cut into flower shapes. Peel the taro and cut into bite size. Boil until tender in salted water, rinse in cold water and drain. Peel the lotus root and burdock root and cut into the same size as the taro. Boil until tender in water to which has been added a little vinegar, rinse in cold water and drain. Cut the small end of the bamboo shoots 2 in. from the end. Cut this into 3 equal pieces from the point. Using the point as the center, cut from the opposite end so that the bamboo shoots form a fan shape as shown in the picture. Cut the remaining bomboo shoots into bite size squares. Cut the *konnyaku* into bite size squares, bring to a boil, rinse in cold water and drain. Cut the broiled soy bean curd into bite size squares. Soften the dried mushrooms in cold water and remove the hard stems.

String the string beans and remove the ends. Drop the string beans into boiling salted water and boil until tender, being careful not to lose the green color, rinse in cold water and drain. Mix $1/3$ t. salt, $2/3$ t. sugar and monosodium glutamate and stir gently until the string beans are well coated.

Mix $2^{1}/_{2}$ cups of the dried young sardine soup stock, 3 T. *mirin*, 1 T. soy sauce, 2 t. salt and $1^{1}/_{2}$ T. sugar and bring to a boil. Add the radish, carrots and taro. Cook until well flavored. Drain the liquid and save to use again. Add the broiled soy bean curd to the liquid and cook until well flavored. Remove the broiled soy bean curd and add 2 T. soy sauce, 2 T. *mirin*, 1 T. sugar, lotus root, burdock root, bamboo shoots, *konnyaku* and dried mushrooms to the liquid. Cook until the vegetables are well flavored. Drain and save the liquid, add the sardines to the liquid and boil until it is almost evaporated.

When all the vegetables have been boiled, mix together lightly, place in the box as pictured and garnish with pine needles.

4. Sunomono, Salads—4th box

a. Chrysanthemum Shaped Turnips

> $1^{1}/_{3}$ lbs. turnips
> 1 lemon
> 10 chrysanthemum leaves
> vinegar
> salt
> sugar
> monosodium glutamate

Cube the turnips ($4/5$ in.) and make very thin slices from the top $3/4$ of the way to the bottom. Slice similarly perpendicularly. Salt and allow to stand until soft. Gently squeeze liquid out. Sprinkle 2 T. vinegar over the turnips and squeeze once more. Mix 4 T. vinegar, $1^{1}/_{2}$ t. salt, $1^{1}/_{2}$ T. sugar and monosodium glutamate (*sanbaizu*). Add the turnips and allow to stand for several hours. Wash the chrysanthemum leaves and spread in the box as shown in the picture, add the flower shaped turnips and in the center of each "flower", add a small piece of lemon rind.

b. Vinegared Shrimp

> 30 shrimp
> vinegar

salt
sugar
monosodium glutamate

Devein the shrimp and boil in salted water until tender. Cool, drain and remove the head, tail and shell. Mix 4 T. vinegar, 1 1/2 t. salt, 1 T. sugar and monosodium glutamate. Marinate the shrimp in this solution for several hours. Drain. Place in the box as shown in the picture.

INDEX

The foods marked * are exported from Japan to America.

*Aburage
    fried soy bean curd
    Soup with cabbage and fried soy bean curd (26)   Soup with ground soy beans and fried soy bean curd (27)   *Inari no hosomaki* (97)   *Kishimen* (122)

Apple
    Fried pork and apple balls (118)

*Azuki-sarashian
    red bean powder
    Mizuyokan (126)   *Ohagimochi* (126)   *Kinakomochi* (127)   *Sakura-mochi* (128)   *Kushi dango* (128)   Chestnut sweets (129)   *Azuki kinton* (132)

Baking soda
    Peony shrimp soup (16)

*Bamboo shoot
    Wakame seaweed soup (21)   Broiled eggplant and eel sandwich (50)   Steamed egg custard (61)   Cuttlefish and bamboo shoot salad (68)   *Takenoko meshi* (86)   *Makunouchi bento* (89)   *Chirashi sushi* (102)   *Karibayaki* (112)   *Sukiyaki* (106)   *Yosenabe* (113)   *Osechi* (136)

Bean sprout
    Soboro-jiru (20)   Pork with persimmon dressing (116)

Beef
    Skewer nibblers (78)   *Soboro donburi* (84)   *Sukiyaki* (106)   *Karibayaki* (112)   Beef and burdock (118)

Beefsteak plant
    Tsukimi somen (121)   *Soroe somen* (121)

*Black sesame seed
    Sekihan (80)

Bofu leaf
    a kind of parsnip
    Spring fish festival (33)

*Bracken
    edible fern sprout
    Peony shrimp soup (16)   Bracken with soy bean curd dressing (41)

Bread
    Hakata tomato (41)

Bread crumbs
    Tobadofu (73)   Skewer nibblers (78)

*Broiled soy bean curd
    Sukiyaki (106)   *Yasainabe*, Vegetables (111)   *Osechi* (136)

Brussel sprout
    Skewer nibblers (78)

*Burdock root
    Japanese *gobo*, common vegetable
    Noppei-jiru (23)   Fried vegetables (77)   Rice and vegetables (86)   *Makunouchi bento* (89)   Beef and burdock (118)   *Osechi* (136)

Cabbage
    Soup with cabbage and fried soy bean curd (26)   Cabbage and ham salad (119)

Carrot
    Pork and vegetable soup (18)   *Kenchin-jiru* (22)   *Noppei-jiru* (23)   *Satsuma-jiru* (28)   Steamed egg custard (61)   "Maple"

salad (64) Fried vegetables (77) *Soboro donbri* (84) Rice and vegetables (86) *Chirashi sushi* (102) *Sukiyaki* (106) *Ni-komi oden* (108) *Yasainabe*, Vegetables (111) Pork with persimmon dressing (116) *Gu somen* (120) *Dango-jiru* (124) *Osechi* (136)

*Chasoba	a kind of vermicelli, made of buckwheat flour and *matcha* (green tea) *Yamakake soba-mushi* (124)
Cheese	Skewer nibblers (78)
*Chestnut	Sweet boiled chestnuts (32) Chestnut sweets (129)
Chicken	How to make soup stock No. 6 (12) Chicken and mushroom soup (17) Chicken and *somen* soup (18) *Zoni* (19) *Noppei-jiru* (23) *Chawan-mushi* (24) *Satsuma-jiru* (28) Spiced chicken (31) Chicken *oharame* (42) Broiled chicken (47) Broiled chicken and mushrooms (48) Roast chicken (48) Three colored rice (83) *Oyako donburi* (85) *Tori gayu* (88) *Makunouchi bento* (89) Chicken rice (93) Decorated *sushi* (98) *Mizutaki* (107) *Nikomi oden* (108) *Yosenabe* (113) *Gu somen* (120) *Odamaki-mushi* (123) *Magatama dango* (133)
*Chikuwa	broiled fish cake, made of fish fillet *Noppei-jiru* (23)
Chrysanthemum	*Tempura* (71)
*Chu-miso paste	made from soy beans, salt and rice malt, seasoning for *miso* soup Soup with cabbage and fried soy bean curd (26) Soup with taro and radish (26)
*Cockle	Instead of this a bloody clam is used. Spring fish festival (33) *Nigiri sushi* (92)
*Cornstarch	Steamed foods (61)
Crab meat	Cucumber and crab meat salad (69)
Crushed Japanese pepper	This is used for cooking with scent.
Cucumber	Stuffed cucumber stew (56) Cucumber and shrimp (64) "Maple" salad (64) Cucumber and crab meat salad (69) Decorated *sushi* (98) *Yoshino sushi* (115)
*Cuttlefish	Instead of this a squid is used. Spring fish festival (33) Sea bream and cuttlefish (36) Cuttlefish and bamboo shoot salad (68) *Tempura* (71) *Tendon* (82) *Nigiri sushi* (94)
Dried brook trout	*Yudofu* (110)
*Dried gourd	*Norimaki sushi* (95) *Inari no hosomaki* (97) *Sushi* sandwiches (100) *Chirashi sushi* (102) *Yushiki sushi* (103)
Dried mushroom	*Kenchin-jiru* (22) *Urauchi shiitake* (39) *Norimaki sushi* (95) Decorated *sushi* (98) *Sushi* sandwiches (100) *Chirashi sushi* (102) *Yushiki sushi* (103) *Yosenabe* (113) *Osechi* (136)
*Dried plum	dried pickled plum *Wakame* seaweed soup (21)
Dried prune	Decorated *sushi* (98)
*Dried shrimp	using for soup stock Soup stock from dried shrimp (No. 4) (12)

*Dried young sardine	using for soup stock Soup stock from dried young sardines (No. 5) (12)
Edible (food) coloring	red, green and blue *Sekihan* (80) *Nishoku yokan* (131) *Wakataketo* (135)
Edible *konbu* seaweed	*Yushiki sushi* (103)
*Eel	Bamboo shoot and eel sandwich (48) Broiled eggplant and eel sandwich (50) *Unadama-mushi* (63)
Egg	Egg and greens soup (14) Egg custard soup (16) *Chawan-mushi* (24) Spring fish festival (33) *Tazuna sushi* (37) *Hakata* tomato (41) Broiled white fish fillet garnished with egg yolk (45) Steamed egg custard (61) *Unadama-mushi* (63) " Maple " salad (64) Three colored rice (83) *Oyako donburi* (85) *Tamago zosui* (87) *Makunouchi bento* (89) Chicken rice (93) *Nigiri sushi* (94) *Norimaki sushi* (95) Decorated *sushi* (98) *Sushi* sandwiches (100) *Chirashi sushi* (102) *Yushiki sushi* (103) *Yosenabe* (113) Scrambled eggs (115) *Irotsukedofu* (117) *Tsukimi somen* (121) *Odamaki-mushi* (123) *Yamakake soba-mushi* (124) *Awayukikan* (127) *Datemaki tamago* (132) Flounder with egg sauce (134) Flower shaped egg (134)
Eggplant	Soup with eggplant (27) Broiled eggplant and eel sandwich (50) Eggplant dressed with mustard (65) Spiced eggplant (66)
Flounder	Checker fish (35) Flounder with egg sauce (134)
Fresh ginger	Sea bream crown with a ginger brush (46)
Frying oil	Fried foods (71)
*Ganmodoki	fried soy bean curd and vegetables *Nikomi oden* (108)
*Ginger	Sweet pickled shrimp (30)
*Gingko nut	*Chawan-mushi* (24) *Noppei-jiru* (23) *Matsuba ginnan* (135)
Green *nori* seaweed	a kind of laver, green laver Skewer nibblers (78)
Green onion	Soy bean curd soup (22) Green onions and round clams (66) *Sukiyaki* (106) *Chirinabe* (109) *Yasainabe*, Vegetables (111)
Green peas	*Noppei-jiru* (23) *Chirashi sushi* (102)
Green pepper	Skewer nibblers (78)
Ham	Radish and ham golden *miso* salad (67) Decorated *sushi* (98) *Sushi* sandwiches (100) Cabbage and ham salad (119)
Hanpen	steamed fish cake, made of white fish fillet, rice flour, *yamaimo*, salt and *mirin* *Nikomi oden* (108)
*Harusame	made from soy bean powder, like noodle Fried shrimp (77) *Yosenabe* (113)
Horseradish	Spring fish festival (33) Checker fish (35) *Nigiri sushi* (94)
Japanese pepper sprout	Clear soup (14)
*Kamaboko	steamed fish cake, made of white fish fillet, salt, *mirin* and cornstarch

141

	Zoni (19) *Chawan-mushi* (24) *Norimaki sushi* (95) *Chirashi sushi* (102) *Odamaki-mushi* (123)
Kanten agar-agar	made of seaweed, dried Spring fish festival (33) Molded *kanten* (41) *Mizuyokan* (126) *Awayukikan* (127) *Nishoku yokan* (131) *Wakataketo* (135)
Karo syrup	Bamboo shoot and eel sandwich (48) *Ohagimochi* (126) Chestnut sweets (129)
Katsuobushi	dried bonito fillet, using for soup stock How to make soup stock No. 1, 2, 3 (11)
Konbu seaweed	using for soup stock How to make soup stock No. 1, 2, 3 (11).
Konnyaku	made from the starch of a tuberous root called "devil's tongue" *Noppei-jiru* (23) *Nikomi oden* (108) *Yasainabe*, Vegetables (111) *Osechi* (136)
Lemon	Bamboo shoot and eel sandwich (48)
Lemon essence	*Awayukikan* (127)
Lettuce	Fried salmon balls (75) Fried pork and apple balls (118)
Lobster	Boiled lobster (52)
Lotus root	Spring fish festival (33) *Jakago renkon* (40) *Chirashi sushi* (102) *Osechi* (136)
Mackerel	Fish with seven spices (74) Boiled mackerel (119)
Matsutake mushroom	a kind of mushroom Chicken and mushroom soup (17) Soy bean curd soup (22) Broiled *matsutake* mushrooms (31) *Karibayaki* (112)
Metade	smartweed Spring fish festival (33) Checker fish (35)
Mirin	sweet rice wine, used for seasoning, made from *sake*, cooked *mochi* rice and rice malt
Mochi rice	glutinous rice *Sekihan* (80) *Ohagimochi* (126) *Kinakomochi* (127)
*Monosodium glutamate	*Ajinomoto*
*Mussel	*Tempura* (71) Skewer nibblers (78) *Yosenabe* (113)
Mustard	Eggplant dressed with mustard (65)
Nama-age	half fried soy bean curd Boiled vegetables (53)
Naruto	steamed fish cake, made of white fish fillet. *Yosenabe* (113)
Nori seaweed	a kind of laver, purple laver Spring fish festival (33) Checker fish (35) Chicken *oharame* (42) Skewer nibblers (78) *Nigiri sushi* (94) *Norimaki sushi* (95) *Sushi* sandwiches (100)
Okara	soy bean curd leftovers *Yoshino sushi* (115)
Olive	Decorated *sushi* (98)

142

143

	Tempura (71) Skewer nibblers (78)
*Sea bream	Instead of this a scup or snapper is used.
	Spring fish festival (33) Sea bream and cuttlefish (36) Broiled sea bream (43) Sea bream crown with a ginger brush (46) *Nigiri sushi* (94)
Sea-eel	*Tempura* (71) Skewer nibblers (78)
*Sea urchin	Cuttlefish and bamboo shoot salad (68)
Senbei	salted Japanese cracker
	Senbei (cracker) *Tempura* (76)
*Shirataki	*konnyaku* cut into strips
	Rice and vegetables (86) *Sukiyaki* (106)
*Shirataki somen	a kind of vermicelli This is very thin.
	Gu somen (120) *Tsukimi somen* (121)
Shiratama powder	treated rice powder; 1 part *mochi* rice powder and 1 part rice powder
	Awayukikan (127) *Sakuramochi* (128)
Shrimp	Peony shrimp soup (16) *Chawan-mushi* (24) Sweet pickled shrimp (30) *Tazuna sushi* (37) *Urauchi shiitake* (39) Broiled salted shrimp (47) Cucumbers and shrimp (64) "Maple" salad (64) *Tempura* (71) Fried shrimp (77) Skewer nibblers (78) *Tendon* (82) *Nigiri sushi* (94) Decorated *sushi* (98) *Chirashi sushi* (102) *Yushiki sushi* (103) *Makunouchi bento* (89) *Nikomi oden* (108) *Yosenabe* (113) Vinegared shrimp (137)
Shungiku	edible chrysanthemum leaf
	Tempura (71) *Sukiyaki* (106) *Chirinabe* (109) *Gu somen* (120)
*Sillago	*Tazuna sushi* (37) *Tempura* (71) Skewer nibblers (78) *Tendon* (82)
*Snipe fish	Spring fish festival (33)
Somen	a kind of vermicelli This is very thin.
	Chicken and *somen* soup (18) *Soroe somen* (121)
Soy bean	Soup stock from vegetables (No. 8) (13) Soup with ground soy beans and fried soy bean curd (27) *Zazen mame* (117)
*Soy bean curd	Soup with *amazake* (sweet wine) and soy bean curd (29) *Niheijiru* (20) Vegetable stew (22) Soy bean curd soup (22) *Gizeidofu* (39) Bracken with soy bean curd dressing (42) Stuffed squash (62) Pork and string bean salad (69) *Ganmodoki* (73) *Tobadofu* (73) *Soboro donburi* (84) *Chirinabe* (109) *Yudofu* (110) *Irotsukedofu* (117)
*Soy bean powder	*Kinakomochi* (127) *Kushi dango* (128)
Soy sauce	*Kikkoman*
Spikenard	like asparagus
	Spring fish festival (33)
Spinach	Egg custard soup (16) Soup with pork and spinach (28) Steamed fish fillet (61) Spinach with white sesame seeds (68) *Norimaki sushi* (95) *Makunouchi bento* (89) *Joyanabe* (107) *Yosenabe* (113)
*String bean	String beans (32) Sea bream and cuttlefish (36) Pork and

	string bean salad (69)
*Sweet boiled bean	Sweet boiled beans (32)
Sweet potato	Fried vegetables (77)
*Taro	a starchy tuberous root
	Noppei-jiru (23) Soup with taro and radish (26) *Satsuma-jiru* (28) *Makuouchi bento* (89) *Nikomi oden* (108) *Yasai nabe*, Vegetables (111) *Dango-jiru* (124) *Osechi* (136) *Osechi* (136)
Tazukuri	dried young sardines This is only used for New year's day festival dishes.
*Tigar lily bulb	lily root, like onion
	Chawan-mushi (24)
Tomato	*Hakata* tomato (41)
Trefoil	greens with 3 leaves
	Egg and greens soup (14) *Zoni* (19) Steamed egg custard (61) *Tempura* (71)
*Tuna fish	Spring fish festival (33) Checker fish (35) *Nigiri sushi* (94)
Turnip	Soup with turnips (27) Steamed fish fillet (61) *Yasainabe*. Vegetables (111) Chrysanthemum shaped turnips (137)
Udo	See spikenard.
Udon	uncooked spaghetti
	Kishimen (122) *Odamaki-mushi* (123)
Ugu	Agar-agar treated green
	Checker fish (35)
Vinegar	*Sunomono* (64)
Wakame seaweed	a kind of seaweed, dried
	Wakame seaweed soup (21)
Wasabi	horseradish
	Sashimi (33) *Sushi* (94)
Wheat flour	*Tempura* (71) Fried vegetables (77) Skewer nibblers (78) *Dango-jiru* (124) *Sakuramochi* (128)
*White baid fish	lancelet
	Wakame seaweed soup (21) Rice and vegetables (86)
White fish fillet	White fish chowder (23) Broiled white fish fillet garnished with egg yolk (45) How to boil white fish fillet (60) Steamed fish fillet (61) *Makunouch bento* (89) *Chirinabe* (109) *Date-maki tamago* (132)
White kidney bean	*Makunouchi bento* (89) *Kushi dango* (128) *Azuki kinton* (132)
White *miso* paste	made from soy bean, salt and rice malt, used for *miso* soup
	Miso cured fish (45) Green onions and round clams (66)
*White sesame seed	Spinach with white sesame seeds (68)
Worcestershire sauce	Skewer nibblers (78)
Yamaimo	Japanese yam
	Nihei-jiru (20) *Yamakake soba-mushi* (124) *Nishoku yokan* (131)

Yamabukizu	sweet vinegar *Sushi* rice (81)
Yellowfish	Broiled yellowfish with sauce (134)
Young *konosirus*	*Chirashi sushi* (102)
Yuzu	a kind of grapefruit In this book lemon is used instead of *yuzu*
Zingiber mioga (Lat.) flower	*Tsukimi somen* (121)